DEREK PIGGOTT ON
GLIDING

By the same author

Beginning Gliding: The Fundamentals of Soaring Flight
Gliding: A Handbook on Soaring Flight
Going Solo: A Complete Guide to Soaring
Understanding Gliding: The Principles of Soaring Flight
Understanding Flying Weather

DEREK PIGGOTT ON
GLIDING

A & C Black · London

First published 1990 by
A & C Black (Publishers) Limited
35 Bedford Row, London WC1R 4JH

© 1990 Derek Piggott

ISBN 0 7136 5799 5

A CIP catalogue record for this book is
available from the British Library.

Printed in Great Britain by
Hollen Street Press Ltd, Slough, Berkshire

Contents

Acknowledgements

I would like to thank Maria Boyd for the original suggestion for this book and for all the help and encouragement she gave me.

Chapters 2–11, 13, 14 and 16 were first published in the British Gliding Association magazine *Sailplane and Gliding*.

Chapter 12 was first published in *The British Soaring Handbook*.

I would like to thank all the editors of these magazines for their help and permission to republish these articles.

Preface

This book brings together material which I think will be useful to instructors and to those gliding enthusiasts who have taken up gliding more recently.

Much of the text is also relevant to flying ultra light aircraft such as the three axis microlights (including Shadow, Thruster, Chevron and so on). Because of their relatively low flying speeds the handling characteristics of these aircraft are usually similar to those of gliders and motor gliders. Moreover, like glider pilots, their pilots must be aware of the effects of turbulence and sinking air.

Throughout the book glider pilots are referred to individually as 'he'. This should, of course, be taken to mean 'he or she' where appropriate.

Units

In most other fields the metric system is used for distances, speeds and weights. However, this is by no means the rule in English speaking gliding circles. Wing spans are always referred to in metres while distances, height gains and speeds for badge and record flights are always referred to in kilometres, metres and kilometres per hour. Rates of climb and flying speeds are usually referred to in knots or nautical miles per hour and most altimeters are calibrated in feet.

It is often useful to know the average achieved rate of climb by timing the gain of height over a period of one or two minutes to obtain the rate of climb in knots or hundreds of feet per minute. As a nautical mile is 6,080 feet, a knot is, for practical purposes, 100 feet per minute.

If flying with an airspeed of 60 knots and the rate of sink indicated is 4 knots, the gliding angle is easy to calculate: 60/4 = 15:1 (in no wind conditions). To make a similar calculation using an airspeed of 110 k.p.h. and sink of 2 metres per second involves converting both to a common time base, say minutes. This is certainly beyond the average pilot in flight without a pocket calculator.

A further advantage is that one minute of latitude always equals one nautical mile, making it easy to measure the distances without having to unfold the map to refer to the normal distance scale.

Introduction

A history of gliding

People have been thinking about ways of flying for thousands of years. The Chinese had their kites but as far as is known kite flying did not progress beyond lifting people for fun and, in time of war, for observation purposes.

Sir George Cayley is now recognised for his work in designing and developing practical gliders. He was the first person to realise that there was no future in having flapping wings like the birds. In 1799 he saw that the wings had to be rigid and the propulsion achieved separately and not by flapping the wings themselves.

Certainly he seems to have established most if not all the essentials necessary for successful flight. He understood streamlining, the need for cambered aerofoils, the need for a proper tail and fin for stability and the use of dihedral on the wings for lateral stability. His model glider designs have proved to be excellent, stable flying machines, and no one seriously doubts that he did indeed put his coachman on a glider to fly a short distance some fifty years before the Wright brothers.

Next came a series of fliers, among them Lilienthal and Pitcher, who developed what are now called hang gliders. Control was achieved mainly by weight shift, and flights of up to a minute became possible.

The Wright brothers then took up the challenge of the conquest of the air and they recognised the need to learn to fly before attempting to build a powered aircraft. Over a period of several years they taught themselves to fly their gliders, developing their machines until they were controllable. By flying in front of a slope in a strong wind they were able to soar for a few seconds and to develop the expertise necessary to fly powered machines at a later date. By that time, petrol engines had been developed and a light enough engine could be made to power the Wright brothers' powered aircraft.

When the 1914–18 war came the development of the practical aeroplane proceeded very rapidly. There was little or no call for gliders during the war, but the Treaty of Versailles, which specifically prohibited the Germans from building and flying powered aircraft, sparked off the idea of their flying gliders instead.

The 1920s saw a very rapid development of glider design, particularly in Germany. At first even a few minutes' flight was a triumph, but soon the records stood at several hours and distance flying had also begun. Using the lift created by the wind blowing up the slopes of hills, and later with the lift under shower clouds, it was not long before flights of hundreds of kilometres were being achieved, not for commercial or military reasons but because it was fun to fly and explore the atmosphere.

Again a war intervened, but this time troop-carrying gliders played their part and in Germany the sporting gliders were used for the basic training of pilots for the German Air Force. In this way a certain amount of glider development continued and many people were introduced to the sport of soaring.

With the return of peace, glider manufacture restarted and gliding clubs re-formed all over the world. Prior to about 1950 almost all glider training was by the solo method. With this students literally taught themselves to fly, starting with ground slides where all they had to do was try to keep straight and hold the wings level on a very crude open frame Primary glider. Later they would progress to low hops and then high hops where the student was launched by car or winch to about 200 feet before gliding down to a landing straight ahead. The flights were measured in seconds and a solo hop of thirty seconds entitled the pilot to the coveted 'A' gliding certificate and badge. Longer flights were usually made by using hill lift although thermals were understood and used by the more experienced pilots.

By 1950 it had generally been recognised that training in dual control two-seater gliders was far more efficient and safe. Well designed two-seater trainers became available all over the world and training by the solo method ceased.

Both the glider pilots and the gliders themselves improved in performance, making much longer flights possible. Wartime developments such as the low drag aerofoils used on the Mustang fighter and other more modern machines attracted the attention of the glider designers. Once adopted, the so-called laminar flow aerofoils resulted in a leap in performance particularly at the faster gliding speeds, making cross-country flying against quite strong winds a possibility. The stiffer wings resulting from the smoother, thick skins necessary for these wing sections also gave an improvement in the lateral control. On many of the earlier designs the wings had obviously been twisting as the ailerons were applied to roll the glider with the result that the aileron effectiveness was diminished.

Today the state of the art is that we have both single and two-seater gliders with gliding angles approaching sixty to one, capable of flights of over 1,000 kilometres (620 miles) at average speeds of nearly 150 k.p.h. (90 m.p.h.). The gliders themselves are almost all made of glass and carbon fibre composites, are simple and safe to fly and incredibly strong. Unfortunately, they are also very expensive to make and buy.

Gliding awards

Without a doubt the progress gliding has made has been greatly influenced by the system of national and international awards. These are recognised throughout the world and set standards of achievement for every glider pilot. At each stage of the pilot's experience there is always another test of skill just within reach.

There are no gliding licences in the UK and the standards are set and maintained by the British Gliding Association. A medical certificate is not required but each pilot has to sign a declaration that he does not suffer from any illness which might make him unfit to fly. In most other countries licences and medical examinations are required.

National awards

The 'A', 'B' and Bronze 'C'

The 'A' and 'B' certificate awards are awarded for the first solo flight and the first soaring flight. Each country has slightly different requirements.

In the UK, and more recently in the USA, there is a Bronze 'C' badge. The requirements for the British Gliding Association Bronze 'C' include a written ground examination on the principles of flight, airmanship, simple meteorology and air law, two soaring flights of a minimum of thirty minutes from a winch or car launch, or one hour from a 2,000-foot aerotow, fifty solo flights and a flying test by a senior instructor. This test includes a simulated field landing or some training in selecting and approaches into fields in a motor glider. Most beginners obtain their Bronze 'C' during their first few months of solo flying.

Fédération Aéronautique Internationale

Silver 'C'

The Silver 'C' badge has three tests or legs.

1. Duration. A soaring flight of over five hours.
2. Gain of height. A gain of height from the lowest point after a release of 1,000 metres (3,281 feet).
3. Distance. A flight of over 50 kilometres (31 miles). This can be done in a variety of ways but in all the loss of height from release to the point of landing or the declared finish point must not exceed one per cent of the total distance.

Whereas in the 1950s the Silver 'C' was considered a very high standard and quite difficult to obtain, in a modern glider the requirements can now be achieved on a single flight. In good conditions the distance flight can be made following a single high climb after release. However, the badge still represents a considerable achievement and gives the pilot status and a substantial reduction in the flying requirement for a Private Pilots' Power Licence.

Gold 'C'

The Gold 'C' badge award also has three legs.

1.   A duration flight of over 5 hours. (In most cases the pilot has done this already for the Silver 'C'.)
2.   A gain of height of 3,000 metres (9,843 feet).
3.   A distance flight of 300 kilometres (186 miles).

Diamond 'C'

There are three diamond awards.

1.   The diamond height. A gain of height of 5,000 metres (16,404 feet).
2.   The diamond for a declared flight of over 300 kilometres (186 miles). (Only an out and return or triangular course declared prior to take-off.)
3.   The diamond distance flight. A flight of over 500 kilometres (311 miles). This can be a flight round up to three different turning points declared before take-off, or a straight distance. (The exact requirements are laid down by the FAI and are somewhat complex.)

More recently flights of over 1,000 kilometres (620 miles) have become relatively common in countries where the soaring conditions are better than in the UK. This has led to the FAI awarding diplomas for both 750 and 1,000 kilometre (465 and 620 mile) flights. To date there have been a few flights of over 750 kilometres in England but none of 1,000 kilometres.

Of course all these flights have to be correctly documented, using a barograph to record the heights and progress of the flight, and photographic evidence to prove that the glider has reached and turned the previously declared turning points correctly.

The badge system has given glider pilots targets to aim for throughout their early and their later flying. In effect the longer tasks are a race or competition against the elements. The soaring conditions normally depend on the effects of the sun's heat and last a maximum of eight or nine hours in the summer-time.

Gliding competitions have played the most important part in the improvement in glider design and flying techniques. They attract both the non-technical pilot and the person who is interested in the decision-making which is involved in flying over long distances and at high speeds. Most competitions consist of a series of races around predetermined turning points so that all the competitors are attempting the same task. Winners of the National Championships are selected to fly in the

World Championships which are held every other year in a different country each time.

Learning to fly gliders

There are gliding clubs and schools in almost every country in the world where a beginner can learn to fly. The first thing to do if you are thinking of taking up the sport is to find where your nearest gliding club or school is located. Ask any gliding enthusiast or, failing all else, contact your National Gliding Association. (*See* Useful Addresses page 157.)

It is usually possible to arrange for a trial flight or introductory lesson to see if you really enjoy it. If there are several clubs within reach, I would suggest visiting them all to see which offers the best opportunities for you. A small 'weekend' club is unlikely to have the facilities of a larger, full-time operation but may be more personal and fun to fly with. If you are able to fly on weekdays, the airfield is bound to be less congested than at weekends, and this will make it easier for early training.

Courses

Many of the larger clubs run residential courses and these provide better continuity than is possible flying on a 'casual' basis. Statistics prove conclusively that, if you can afford it, formal courses are more efficient and, in the end, less costly than flying now and again with a different instructor each time. If you do decide to start with a course it is worth while trying to get one or two flights beforehand to acclimatise. Many students start their course with virtually no experience and find it difficult to get relaxed until the week is nearly over.

It is impossible to state exactly how long it takes to learn to reach solo standard. However, it is true to say that beyond 30, the older you are the more experience it will take. For most pilots it takes 2 or 3 weeks of continuous training or about 6–8 hours and 50–60 flights. This can easily run up to 80–90 flights if you fly on an occasional basis because you soon forget and get out of practice.

Usually you fly with your instructor to practise every conceivable emergency until you are both confident of your ability to fly safely. As well as stalling and spinning, launch failures and cable break procedures, every aspect of flying will be covered. It is usual to make the first solo flights in the two-seater glider that you are training on, and for dual training to continue with daily check flights, until you have ten to twenty solo flights behind you.

Incidentally, modern two-seater gliders are capable of good soaring performances, and by the time you are ready to solo it is normal for you to have learned how to use thermals. Even on your first solo flights you may be able to stay up for half an hour in good conditions.

Private ownership

Until they have reached about Bronze 'C' standard the vast majority of pilots use club single-seater gliders. This means being at the field early on any promising soaring day in order to get your name near the top of the flying list. Usually the order of the list is the order for flying, so first come, first to fly. This is reasonably satisfactory for the pilot who is building up experience during the winter months, but for the enthusiast who wants to be able to stay up most of the day, it is very frustrating to be at the bottom of the flying list and to find all the club machines up soaring. It is a great advantage to own a share in a glider so that you can fly more and do not have to bother with the flying list system.

Most gliders are owned by syndicates of up to six pilots with proper agreements as to how the glider is shared between the members. Gliders do not depreciate much in value and used gliders are often changing hands as their owners get the urge to move on to machines with a higher performance. The maintenance is minimal and the major cost is the insurance. Most pilots insure their gliders comprehensively, although they are only legally liable to insure for third party risks. Owning a share in a glider is essential if you are ambitious and want to progress quickly.

Is it for you?

Unfortunately gliding is not one of those sports which you can do on an occasional basis. It is essential to practise constantly if you are to fly safely and efficiently. Moreover, it is not an individual sport as it requires team-work to get up in the air. Just to get launched requires a team effort with at least three or four other enthusiasts helping. You need a winch driver or tow pilot, a wing runner and signaller and, except in a commercial gliding school such as exist in the USA, you rely on fellow members and not on paid staff.

To go gliding you really need to set aside the whole day so that you can help others as well as fly yourself. If this puts you off the idea, I'm pleased to have saved you time and money. Most gliding enthusiasts find that they enjoy all the activities and not just the flying. Gliding is for them a way of life.

1   The learning process

While you are learning to glide you are in the midst of a host of problems and difficulties. It is only too easy for an instructor or an experienced pilot to dismiss your anxieties with a comment such as 'Oh, you will soon get the idea – it's just a matter of experience'. Whereas this can be true, it is much quicker and easier to tackle each difficulty by understanding why it happens and how to overcome it rather than to carry on hoping it will all come right in the end.

If you are well on the way to solo you will almost certainly have forgotten the horrible sensations that you experienced on your early flights. When you are just starting to learn you will find these sensations most disconcerting if not alarming. At first they will often prevent you from thinking clearly and controlling the glider properly. But remember that they are quite normal and should disappear gradually as your eyes and other senses get used to flying and are able to tell you what is going on.

Co-ordination – stick and rudder

Certainly the greatest problem is to control your feet so that you can make co-ordinated movements of the stick and rudder as you go into and out of turns. Because you have to form a habit and habits take time and experience to form, you cannot learn this co-ordination out of a book or in any other way except by practice. Remember that straight flight is going to be impossible at first until those movements are almost instinctive and automatic. So, don't get discouraged when you can't even fly straight. Your instructor will not be surprised or disappointed in you as everyone has this problem.

Length of practice sessions

You will also find that this co-ordination will get quite good on one day and then degenerate the next. This happens for a variety of reasons. If you fly for more than about twenty minutes practising turns, you will find them getting worse as you lose concentration. For most beginners, two or three five-minute winch launch flights or one aerotow of about twenty minutes is about the limit for making progress, and then it is best to stop and have a break before doing any more. You will soon realise that in the early stages, long soaring flights do not get you much further towards solo, nor do they teach you much about soaring techniques. Thirty minutes of working hard is worth more than an hour or more when you are getting tired.

Some common problems

The approach

You will often find that your turns go well when you are up flying high but deteriorate as you get lower and begin to think about the approach. As soon as you are flying down towards the landing area the glider seems possessed with the devil and starts to yaw all over the place. Don't despair, this is quite normal. It just means that your co-ordination has not yet reached the automatic stage and that when you start to think about the approach and landing you are forgetting to use the rudder. Each time you make a little sideways movement on the stick to get the wings level, that aileron drag swings the nose off to one side. Don't worry. In a few more flights' time the problem will cure itself and all will be well.

Confidence

You may even find it difficult to get the glider to fly where you want on the circuit. Once again the cause is too much to think about so that the rudder movements get forgotten.

Ultimately, it is important to understand what is making the glider behave as its does, particularly with respect to stalling and spinning. Don't be afraid to ask questions if you don't understand something. It can all be explained in simple terms and you ought to be apprehensive about things until you understand how and why they are happening. Even then you need experience and practice to gain confidence in your ability to deal with any situation which might arise. Confidence without understanding can be very dangerous in all forms of flying.

Landings

Landings always seem much more difficult than they really are because each one is different. Once you understand what you are trying to do you begin to have a chance of learning how, but any misunderstanding guarantees that problems will arise. If you are already having difficulty, look at a copy of my book *Beginning Gliding* which has a very comprehensive section on how to learn to land.

Airbraking

Things often begin to go wrong when you start to use the airbrakes, and your progress may be held up. Until then you will probably only have had problems with co-ordination. Suddenly you are expected to use judgements which seem vague and undefinable. Once again a better understanding will be a great help. Get your instructor to explain how to judge the circuit and approach.

Following the towplane

You are almost certain to find that following the towplane on aerotow gives you problems at first. Do not despair. It is just a knack which comes suddenly after a certain amount of practice. I have never known anyone who could not learn to do it, so I am sure you will not be an exception.

Planning the approach

When it comes to planning and judgement, remember that it is much easier to get a good approach if you have a reasonably long base leg. This gives you more time to think and adjust your positioning for the final turn. It is a mistake to try to arrive with a minimum of height for the base leg and final turn as this seldom leaves you enough time or room to make adjustments.

You must learn to give yourself enough time to monitor the airspeed, adjust the positioning and height, and open the airbrakes and adjust their setting on the approach. To do this you have to think ahead of the action or you will be so short of time that you will have to make whatever approach you can from the position that the glider has put you into. There are numerous ways in which you can make the planning more difficult for yourself, and consistently being slightly short of height in the pattern is one of the obvious ones.

The same applies for launch failures and other emergencies. You often get an incomplete briefing out on the airfield and some of the things which can and do occasionally happen are very serious unless you know about them beforehand.

Learning anything new is always interesting and learning to fly is a great challenge for most people. The following chapters are designed to help both beginners and instructors to grasp the essentials more quickly.

They do not include all aspects of gliding; for example winch launching and stalling and spinning have been omitted as they are well covered elsewhere and are best introduced by the instructor.

2   First flights

One of the biggest difficulties in learning to glide is convincing yourself that you are, in fact, making satisfactory progress. To do this you must understand a little about the learning process, and this is not often explained by the instructor. It is an unfortunate fact that many quite important aspects of glider training do not always get covered by every instructor. The misunderstandings which arise create problems for everyone and I am hoping that this book will be of help to both students and instructors.

Sensations on your first flight

Few pilots or instructors spare enough time to explain the sensations a beginner usually experiences on the first few flights. At this stage it is quite normal to have worrying if not rather frightening feelings, and many would-be pilots dislike them so much that they give up after one or two flights. A few words of comfort and explanation would be invaluable to most people having their first glider ride.

There are several reasons for these sensations. Our sense of balance is normally directly related to gravity and we are not familiar with movements and accelerations in all three dimensions. Once in the air, therefore, we begin to experience worrying sensations but are unable to relate them to the movements of the aircraft. Such sensations are normally suppressed by our brain when our eyesight recognises exactly what is happening. But this only comes with the experience of a number of flights.

Also, at this stage it is quite normal and only natural to be rather nervous about handling the controls, and this uncertainty adds to our worries. Flying on a turbulent day, and particularly when there is no clear horizon, makes these sensations far worse. There is no way of telling when the bumps will occur and it is more difficult to recognise what is happening to the aircraft as it is tipped or jolted about. When handling the controls in these conditions every bump gives the impression that the aircraft is about to fall out of the sky, and only constant reassurance by the instructor will help a nervous person to enjoy the flight.

We are particularly sensitive at first to the feeling of 'lightness', which occurs as we lower the nose of the glider. This low 'g' or reduced 'g' sensation is similar to the feeling of falling we experience in a nightmare, so we tend to associate it with falling. On an early flight the feeling is alarming because the possibility of falling out of the glider seems very real. After a few more flights your brain anticipates the feeling as you move the stick forward and see the nose actually dropping in relation to the horizon. The same sensation can occur flying through turbulence. In this case we learn to identify the cause and after a number of flights the bumps, although disturbing, cease to alarm us.

Conditions for first flights

The importance of selecting reasonably smooth conditions for your first few flights is obvious. These sensations may continue to be worrying until you have confidence in the use of the controls. Until then it will be frightening to find that the glider is not responding or is momentarily tipping the other way as it is bumped. On a very hazy day it is much more difficult to see what is happening, making the sensations worse and reducing your confidence in what you are doing.

In practice the weather is never perfect, but it is helpful to realise that turbulence and poor visibility are bound to have a big influence on your flying ability and confidence in the early stages. These are very significant problems if you are a beginner, and pilots and instructors concerned with early training flights should, therefore, explain them to avoid prolonged circling, stalling or any abrupt manoeuvres.

Learning the controls

The first real lesson in flying is to find out the effects of controls. You will soon get the hang of the stick movements. If you move the stick forward the nose goes down, while if you move it backwards the nose goes up. Moving the stick a little to the left causes the glider to tip or bank to the left and also to begin to turn. The easy way to remember the sideways stick movements is that you move the stick towards the wing you want to push down, that is you push the wing down with the stick.

But whereas the stick movements are logical and soon become almost instinctive and automatic, no one finds the rudder movements easy or natural. Those rudder movements certainly are the devil to get right! Not only is it a matter of getting the correct direction and amount of movement, but they have got to become almost totally automatic. This is further complicated by the variations in the rudder forces which can occur when your co-ordination is poor. On many types of training gliders, particularly the K7, K13 and Bocian, the rudder tends to 'overbalance' whenever the turns are inaccurate.

Imagine yourself as a beginner trying to learn to turn. Unwittingly you fail to apply quite enough left rudder as you bank over into a turn to the left. Something odd seems to happen and you get a vivid feeling as though the glider is rolling right over and you are going to fall out. Then you feel the rudder pedals move as if the instructor is on the controls. 'Damn it' you think. 'Why can't he leave me alone'. It all becomes even more confusing when you realise that it feels as though he is pushing on the right rudder pedal but he is telling you to apply more left rudder.

This is very confusing until some time later you realise that most of the time your instructor was not even touching the pedals and that it wasn't him but the airflow which was moving the rudder and accentuating your original small error. The reason for this problem is that the rudder on most gliders does not centralise itself. Every time that the aircraft is banked into or out of a turn without the correct amount of rudder, it flies slightly sideways for a few seconds. As this happens the airflow pushes sideways on the rudder surface, moving it further across the wrong way. If you feel the rudder moving or trying to move against your feet it may not be the instructor riding the controls at all. Imagine, if you like, that you have a lunatic sitting in the back cockpit. Every time you get the rudder movement wrong he insists on making your error worse by kicking on the wrong rudder even more. For example if you apply too much rudder or keep it on during the turn instead of reducing it to just a small amount, the aircraft will skid badly and the rudder will overbalance and lock on requiring some force to reduce the deflection or to re-centralise it.

If you experiment and apply full rudder slowly you will notice how to begin with it takes more and more force to apply. Then, quite suddenly the force required drops or even reverses so that the full rudder will stay on by itself. A further confusion often arises. At the same time as the rudder overbalances, the needle of the Air Speed Indicator (ASI) swings back through the zero mark to give an entirely false reading. If you happen to be glancing at it at that moment you may well be deluded into thinking that you are about to stall. Even a small amount of slip or skid will cause the ASI to under-read.

If you do feel this movement of the rudder pedals as though your instructor is riding the controls, ask him. He should be able to tell when the rudder overbalances by watching your turns, and ideally he should tell you when his feet are off the pedals and that the movement you experience is the air moving the rudder and not him.

This characteristic is unacceptable in a normal powered aircraft. It is really caused by a lack of directional stability, that is when the fin is too small. It causes endless confusion to beginners but is scarcely ever noticed by the experienced glider pilot. As a result the effect is often forgotten by instructors or at least not demonstrated in a convincing manner. Get your instructor to show you or try it for yourself.

Make no mistake, this co-ordination of the stick and rudder is the main difficulty in learning to fly gliders. The trouble is that it has to become a habit and almost totally automatic. This takes practice – turns,

turns, and more turns. Note also that you will not be able to fly straight until these movements are correct. For example if a wing drops the glider will start to turn immediately. If you bring the wings level with the stick alone, forgetting the rudder, the adverse yaw will swing you even further off your original heading. To fly straight your correction for a wing dropping has to be immediate and accurately done by co-ordinating the stick and rudder together. Every time that you make a sideways movement on the stick and forget the rudder, the glider will start to swing from side to side.

Do not despair if you cannot do this after a few lessons. Flying straight will probably be one of the last things that you will learn before going solo. You will not be alone in finding this apparently simple exercise difficult.

The attitude

Most glider flying is done by attitude rather than by constantly referring to the ASI. This entails checking the position of the nose in relation to the horizon in order to maintain safe flying speeds. If the nose is in the correct attitude the glider will be cruising efficiently with easy handling. However, if the nose is a little too high the speed will be insufficient to give good control and the rate of descent will be high, while if the nose is too low the glider will be diving at a great speed, losing height rapidly.

After looking around before starting a turn, it is best to look ahead to re-check that the position of the nose is correct. This ensures that any changes in attitude can be spotted immediately. Do not watch the wing-tip.

When there is no horizon the pilot must guess the attitude and refer to the ASI more frequently to check that the speed is correct. However, overconcentrating on the ASI results in flying alternately too slow and too fast, because of the time taken for the aircraft to change speed after a change in attitude. This is known as 'chasing' the airspeed.

3   Turns

Co-ordinating control movements

Once you have seen how each control works, you are confronted with the problem of learning to co-ordinate the stick and rudder to produce accurate turns. Although it might seem that the two controls could be coupled together to work automatically for the movements required, their position in a steady turn with the stick pointing slightly one way and the rudder in the other makes this impractical. So the pilot has to learn a more complicated sequence which takes time and practice to establish.

However, the sequence can be considered as a pattern of movements and learned as such. With the exception of a few vintage machines which may have rather odd handling, the control movements follow a standard pattern. In fact it is often easiest for the instructor to dictate the movements to help to establish them, saying something like the following:

'First look right round and behind, then look ahead. Now stick and rudder together to apply the bank; check (or stop) the bank with the stick

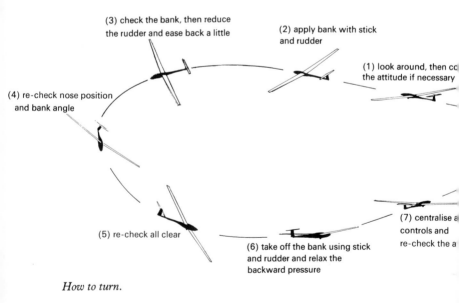

(3) check the bank, then reduce the rudder and ease back a little

(2) apply bank with stick and rudder

(1) look around, then cc the attitude if necessary

(4) re-check nose position and bank angle

(7) centralise a controls and re-check the a

(5) re-check all clear

(6) take off the bank using stick and rudder and relax the backward pressure

How to turn.

and then reduce the rudder; ease back slightly to prevent the nose from dropping; re-check it's still all clear. Coming out of the turn, stick and rudder together and relax the backward pressure on the stick; centralise the stick and rudder together as the wings come level'.

The vital thing is to ensure that the basic movements are correct. Practising the wrong movements will form bad habits which will be very difficult to rectify at a later date. Unfortunately, most gliders will make quite reasonable turns even though some serious faults are being made, and this makes the instructor's task a difficult one. For example it is possible to enter a turn gradually with no aileron movement at all yet without any detectable error. Also, it is almost impossible to spot any skidding in a turn even though the amount of rudder used has not been reduced, especially after a good entry using the stick and rudder correctly. Bad faults like this soon become habits and often are the cause of appallingly bad turns on to the final approach when the bank is applied quickly or a steeper turn becomes necessary.

The rudder

The reason for all this rudder work is simple. As the bank is applied, the rising wing is dragged back so that the nose is swung off and up in the opposite direction to the bank. This occurs because the wing which

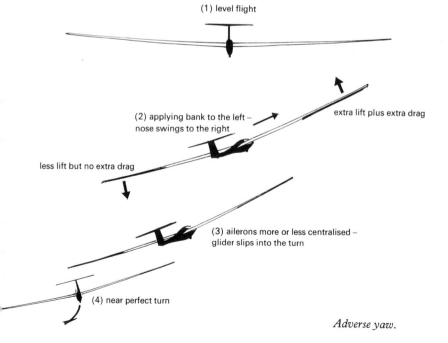

(1) level flight

(2) applying bank to the left – nose swings to the right

extra lift plus extra drag

less lift but no extra drag

(3) ailerons more or less centralised – glider slips into the turn

(4) near perfect turn

Adverse yaw.

provides more lift also creates more drag. Whenever the angle of bank is changed by making one wing develop more lift that the other, the extra drag causes a tendency to swing. This 'yawing' movement only lasts a few seconds but prevents a smooth entry into the turn. The 'adverse yaw' as it is called is exaggerated by the big wing span and low flying speed, making it vital to use the stick and rudder together when applying or taking off the bank. Once in the turn this effect is almost eliminated so that the amount of rudder required is very small.

It takes quite a lot of practice to learn to use the correct amount of rudder, particularly if there is a change of rudder loads or if the airflow moves the rudder in the opposite direction. Trying to 'feel' the amount by following through on the controls as your instructor demonstrates a turn is not much help because it is difficult to sense the amount of rudder being used by feel, and, of course, because while the instructor is on the controls you can get no idea of the force he is having to apply to move it by that amount.

Some common faults with beginners

The following are some suggestions as to what you may be doing wrong if you find that you are never using the rudder correctly. When your feet and leg muscles get very tense, as they do on these early flights, you will tend to push with one foot without remembering to relax and withdraw the other one. When you do this, all you do is stretch the cables without moving the rudder. A few moments of moving the rudder, first one way and then the other, using quite large movements but without worrying about what the glider is doing, will help you to relax and make real movements when you want them.

You may find that you tend to under-rudder more to the right than to the left. This is likely if you are a car driver as your right foot is conditioned to the delicate touch needed for the accelerator. If you fail to use enough rudder going into a turn to the right but still reduce the amount of rudder by a normal amount once the turn is established, you will end up in a right-hand turn with some left rudder. Although not dangerous, this fault creates a very worrying sensation as though the glider is rolling right over and is about to fall out of the sky. The turn ends up sideslipping badly with the wrong rudder still being applied. Watch for this tendency to under-rudder to the right and remind yourself to use enough.

The other helpful thing is to watch the actual control movements as your instructor demonstrates a turn. Hopefully he will make the moves slowly and deliberately and describe them in the process:

'I'll look around this time. Watch the stick and rudder movements and try to memorise how much they move and how I move them. Stick and rudder together – see the amount of rudder. Checking the banking movement with the stick to keep it constant, I then reduce the rudder. See the small amount I leave on for the turn. Now I'm using a small backward movement to prevent the nose from dropping. Coming out of the turn, I move the stick and the rudder exactly together as if I am going to change over to a turn in the other direction. Now as the wings are coming level, I move the stick and the rudder together to centralise the controls'.

The visual image formed by watching the actual movements helps enormously in overcoming the initial difficulties of getting the timing and the amount of the movements correct.

During the early flights most beginners have much the same problems with the use of the rudder. At first it is usually either a failure to use the rudder at all or to use it sufficiently. Later it is more likely to be more subtle faults which are difficult for the instructor to spot and analyse correctly. Often these faults go undetected and they soon become bad habits which are then even more difficult to eliminate. Strange as it may seem, the surest way to detect poor co-ordination habits is for the instructor to watch the control movements as these should follow an easily recognisable pattern.

A lot of problems can occur if all the stick and rudder movements are made simultaneously. The two controls should be moved exactly together as you apply the bank, as you take off the bank and as you centralise the controls to keep the wings level after coming out of a turn. However, it is important to make the stick movement just a little *before* reducing the rudder as the required angle of bank is established. The ailerons are used to roll the aircraft and must be used to stop the banking movement at the angle you want. The rudder must be used as you apply the bank to prevent the adverse yaw, but it does not control the banking. (Of course changing the position of the rudder does have some influence on banking movements because of the effects of dihedral and so on, making the glider tend to bank when the rudder is applied.)

Unfortunately the habit of reducing the rudder at the same moment as the ailerons are moved to stop the banking movement results in repeated side-slipping faults. It is exasperatingly difficult to re-learn the correct movement except by exaggerating the pause between checking the bank with the aileron and reducing the rudder. On balance I believe it is best to teach a definite and deliberate gap to establish the right kind of habit, knowing that with more experience and practice the gap will close. Above all it is most important that the amount of rudder is always reduced once the bank has been established.

Some common faults with power pilots

Power pilots converting to gliders will have almost as much difficulty as a beginner because their habits are already formed and are difficult to change. If asked to make a turn they usually start to apply the bank as they look around, only to find to their annoyance and amazement that on looking forward again the glider is in an unexpected nose-high attitude, slipping badly. Their problems are best solved by the instructor's slowing them down to make them think about the moves instead of allowing them to happen automatically. He may tell them the following: 'Look around, but don't start the turn yet. Now look ahead. Think of the movements – stick and rudder together. Now go into the turn and don't watch the wing-tip.'

In the early stages it is probably a bad thing to attempt to use the yaw string or slip ball to detect or correct errors caused by the wrong amount of rudder. This is because the movements which should become automatic can easily become a series of corrections requiring constant attention from the pilot. In this respect the use of the rudder on a glider is different to that on a powered aircraft. In these machines the rudder is applied as a correction for the yaw which occurs after increasing or decreasing the power to climb or glide. But after the change of power the pilot can afford to wait and observe the resulting yaw before applying the necessary rudder to overcome it. A small amount of slip or skid is relatively unimportant and so it doesn't matter much if the power pilot takes time to detect and correct it. However, with a glider the use of the rudder during the entry to the turn must be automatic. Poor co-ordination makes it impossible to fly straight.

Handling characteristics

The light aeroplane pilot will soon realise that the large wing-span and low flying speed of the glider result in very different handling characteristics to other aircraft. Unlike a light aircraft the stick position in a turn is not central as there is always a tendency for the angle of bank to increase. This increase must be avoided by using the ailerons to 'hold off' the bank. At the same time a small amount of rudder is required in the direction of the turn. This is a 'crossed' control situation which in a normal aircraft would be a sign of over-ruddering.

The amount of hold-off required to keep a constant angle of bank is quite small unless an excess amount of rudder has been left on or unless the glider is flying too slowly and is close to stalling. Both causes can lead to trouble and therefore a large deflection of the aileron to hold off the bank should always be considered as a danger sign. Excess rudder results in skidding and very high drag as the fuselage moves sideways through the air. This acts as an airbrake and inevitably causes a loss of airspeed and a risk of stalling even though the nose has not been raised. There is also a tendency for the glider to overbank more at very low speeds so that a large stick deflection to hold off the bank can also be a warning of a dangerously low speed. In either case, lowering the nose should be the first action, followed by checking the amount of rudder being used and reducing it as necessary.

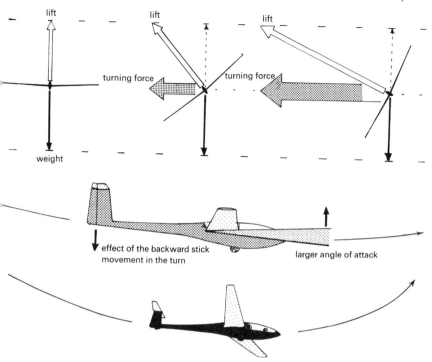

lift

lift

lift

turning force

turning force

weight

effect of the backward stick
movement in the turn

larger angle of attack

*Easing back on the stick after banking over ensures greater turning force. This in
turn pulls the wings to a slightly larger angle of attack, providing the required
amount of extra lift.*

Co-ordination practice

Once the correct movements are becoming established, it is useful to
practise turning smoothly from one direction to the other. Some
instructors try to get their students to 'roll' on a point, that is to bank
from one side to the other without turning. Strictly speaking this should
be impossible, since the glider is being kept straight while it is banked,
an aerodynamic impossibility without some slipping movement. A far
better exercise is to allow the glider to turn and to make some of the
changes in bank quickly and others slowly. It is important to keep some
of the turns going for long enough to ensure that the rudder is reduced
once the turns are established.

Most gliders are extremely short of rudder power and directional
stability. If all the aileron deflection is used to apply the bank very
quickly even full rudder will not eliminate the adverse yaw. It is easier to
limit the amount of aileron movement to half or three quarters of the

available stick movement so that an accurate turn can be made. Once in the turn very little rudder is needed, regardless of the type of aircraft or glider.

In any turn the force required to make the change in direction is obtained by banking over and using the lift from the wings to pull you round the turn. More lift is therefore required and this is obtained by easing back on the stick to pull the wings to a larger angle of attack. The amount of this backward movement is very small for a gentle turn and increases rapidly as the bank is increased beyond about 30°. Since centring in thermals depends on straightening up quickly and turning accurately at a low, controlled speed at varying angles of bank, the ability to apply the correct amount of backward pressure almost instinctively is necessary for efficient soaring. An accurate steep turn at a relatively low speed will often make it possible to use the very narrow cores of lift and so climb much faster.

4   Landings

There is only one real problem about learning to land a glider – you only get one landing per flight. A single flight gives you just one go at making a satisfactory landing and very little, if any, hope of finding out whether that good landing was due to chance or skill. Ideally, you need a number of consecutive landings to make any real progress.

In order to make consistently safe landings you need to learn to recognise what is happening during the landing and to respond with the appropriate control movement. This cannot be done by learning the rate and size of the backward movement on the stick since this will be different for every landing.

Judgement

Difficulties usually arise because of a misconception about what you are supposed to do. For example if you are attempting to land on a particular spot you will always tend to fly the glider on to the ground instead of

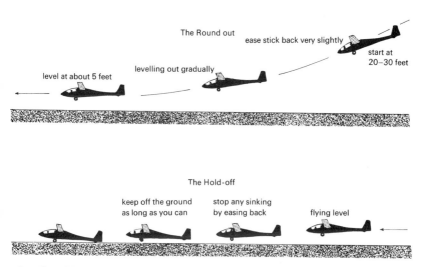

Landing. Make a very tiny, gradual movement on the stick to start the round-out at about 20–30 feet. Then use a gentle backward movement to keep the glider just above the ground until it sinks slightly and lands.

trying to keep it off as long as possible. Similarly, if you are trying to judge the landing attitude you will inevitably fly on to the ground prematurely.

What you should be doing is to gradually level out from the approach so that you are flying more or less level, a few feet above the ground. (This is known as the 'flare out', 'round out', or 'initial check'.) Then you should attempt to keep the aircraft just a few feet above the ground, stopping it from sinking by gradually easing back on the stick. If the aircraft starts to gain height (known as 'ballooning') stop the backward movement, wait until you see that you are beginning to lose height and then ease back to continue the hold-off. Finally the glider will sink on to the ground in spite of your backward movement.

Ballooning

It is only after a few attempts that you become aware of the difficulties. Because of the increased flying speed used on the approach the elevator is extra sensitive so that the initial backward movement has to be very small, perhaps only 2mm (1/16in) or so. Most beginners overdo the initial movement on their first attempts. Unfortunately, as the glider balloons upwards a few feet they will respond instinctively by moving forward on the stick. This will usually result in a very rapid loss of height and a rather heavy premature landing. Hopefully your instructor will be ready for this and will be quick to stop you.

In order to land satisfactorily you will have to learn to overcome that instinct. Unless you balloon upwards twenty or thirty feet you will not have time to avoid flying into the ground if you move forward. Instead, you should hold your hand still, wait, and as you see you are starting to sink again, begin another gentle backward movement on the stick to stop the sink as the glider reaches a height of a few feet. For most people this is easier said than done. It seems almost automatic to make a forward movement, so you will have to unlearn this instinct. Only if the ballooning takes you very high or occurs towards the end of the hold-off is there any need to move forward momentarily. As long as the approach speed has been adequate, the ballooning movement is with the aircraft in an almost level attitude and there is no danger of stalling.

The float or hold-off

Whereas in normal flight the attitude of the aircraft is all-important, during the landing you should cease to worry about the attitude and instead concentrate on your height above the ground. Fortunately the designers of most gliders have set the wing on the fuselage at the correct angle to suit the undercarriage. If the pilot keeps the glider from sinking while flying a foot or two above the ground eventually it will sink and

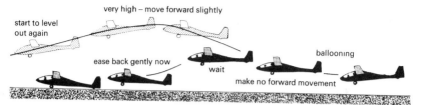

very high – move forward slightly

start to level
out again

ease back gently now

wait

ballooning

make no forward movement

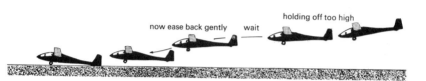

now ease back gently

wait

holding off too high

Ballooning or holding off too high. If ballooning is very high a small movement forward should be made to start a fresh approach. However, unless the height is more than 10–15 feet, hold the stick and wait until the glider starts to sink again. Then hold off with a gradual backward movement until the glider lands.

land itself in spite of his gentle backward movement on the stick. The touch down will then be at a low speed and in a rather tail-down attitude, landing on the main wheel and tail skid more or less simultaneously.

How far the glider floats during this hold-off will vary enormously from landing to landing. Excessive speed or a very small amount of airbrake will result in a longer float and a greater tendency for the pilot to overdo the backward movement and so cause ballooning. Landing against a strong wind or the drag caused by using full airbrake will reduce the distance of the float. Since every approach is at a slightly different angle and speed and the round out is seldom started at the same height, no two landings can ever be exactly similar.

Learning to land is made far easier if the instructor takes over the task of planning the approach and also of using the airbrakes. It is an easy matter for him to make any changes in the airbrake setting to compensate for a slightly lower approach speed or for losing too much speed while ballooning. The ideal for the beginner is that the airbrakes should be kept in a constant position for the final part of the approach and not changed unless it is really necessary. Changing the airbrakes at exactly the right moment as the glider starts to sink again after ballooning takes skill and practice and it saves time to get the landing right first before introducing the airbrakes. At this early stage of learning it is also important to try to arrange every approach so that there is a minimum of about half-airbrake for the final stage. This acts like a reserve of energy since by closing the airbrakes the wings develop more lift and less drag, enabling the glider to fly safely at a lower speed.

Timing

If you leave the initial check or round out until you are a few feet above the ground any slight error in timing will result in flying into the ground. Furthermore, the backward movement needed to round out quickly will have to be a jerk and it will be pure luck if you happen to get the timing and the amount of movement correct. If, on the other hand, you start at twenty or even thirty feet and make the stick movement very gradual, the timing becomes much less critical. In this case the levelling out can be delayed or speeded up slightly as necessary by holding the stick still to allow the machine to sink closer to the ground or by moving back a little more to stop it getting too close. When the aircraft is several feet above the ground and flying more or less level it will start to sink as it loses speed. As it sinks a gradual backward movement on the stick will stop the descent, and this movement should be continued as necessary to prevent the glider landing. Too large a movement or making it too quickly will result in the glider gaining height. If this happens, hold the stick still for a few seconds until the machine starts to sink again, then continue the hold off as long as you can. The glider will make your landing for you.

Looking ahead

From the point of view of learning to land ballooning is actually a good thing. When the glider starts to balloon you can predict what is going to happen next and therefore be ready to make the right move. If you look well ahead you will see immediately that the glider begins to gain height. Hold the stick still. Next, the glider will stop going up and will start to sink again. So all you have to do is to be ready to make that gentle backward movement as you see the glider begin to lose height. In this way you know ahead of time what you will need to do. There is usually plenty of time to spot what is happening and to make the control movements. Do not try to keep too close to the ground during the hold-off. If you try to keep within a few inches like the experts you will always fly on to the ground and land prematurely. You must have enough time to spot that the glider is sinking and to make a move to stop it before it touches the ground, so you need two or three feet and not just a few inches. Later, when you are more experienced, you will notice when the glider sinks only an inch or two and then you will be able to hold off closer to the ground.

At first this ballooning is annoying and rather alarming, but the exaggerated movements up and down help to teach you to detect and recognise what is happening. If you become overanxious about it you are most likely to fly into the ground hard if you happen to start to balloon and respond instinctively. Often the root cause of a lot of these problems is that you are not looking far enough ahead. You need to look about a hundred yards ahead to be able to spot what is happening. If you look just over the nose you will see the ground rushing up towards you at the last moment and you will almost always overcontrol and balloon. A very quick glance sideways during the approach will often enable you to see how high you are in relation to trees or buildings nearby so that you can tell if you are still far too high to start the round out.

Remember, look well ahead; be gentle with the movements; don't leave the initial check late but start gently in plenty of time. Don't try to get too close to the ground. Two or three feet is fine, and then keep it floating as long as you can.

Once you can make fairly consistent, fully held-off landings without the instructor having to change the airbrakes, you are ready to progress to the stage of using the airbrakes and doing the planning yourself.

5 The use of airbrakes

Planning the circuit

In order to simplify learning to land it is easiest if the instructor takes over the whole responsibility of planning the circuit and the approach. In other words, the student is talked round into position with the instructor using the airbrakes as necessary to bring the glider down towards the landing area ready for the landing. It is not even necessary for the student to be aware of their use while he is concerned only with the landing. Once the hold-off and touch down have become fairly consistent and without any uncontrolled ballooning, then it is time to start both using the airbrakes and making the necessary judgements for the whole flight.

A proper understanding of the use of the airbrakes is essential for safe flying. They are not just a landing lever to be used automatically just after the final turn. Their use is not a matter of learning how to operate the lever but rather of when and how much to use in the various situations and conditions which occur. For this reason it is of little value to have a beginner using the airbrakes if the instructor is telling him when and how to use them.

Types of airbrake

There are a number of different types of airbrake in use today but, with the exception of trailing edge brakes such as those used on the Mosquito, Mini Nimbus and Vegas, they all act as lift spoilers as well as increasing the drag. Part of the wing is seriously affected so that it creates less lift and this makes the aircraft behave as though the wings have been clipped. This loss of lift raises the stalling speed, typically by about 2–3 knots. This might be thought of as a slight disadvantage as it means that the touch-down speed using full airbrake is that little bit faster than it would be with them closed. However, this rise in stalling speed is put to good use any time that the glider is ballooned up a few feet during a landing. It makes it possible to avoid a heavy landing by quickly closing the airbrakes partially or fully. This both reduces the drag so that further speed is lost more slowly and increases the lift so that the glider is able to continue flying at a lower speed. This is rather like using a burst of engine power in a light aircraft to prevent a heavy landing, except that

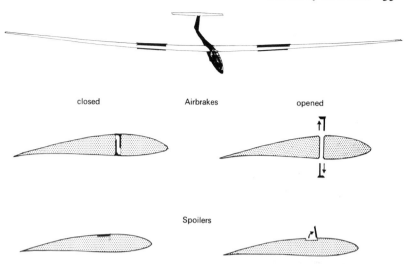

closed   Airbrakes   opened

Spoilers

Airbrakes create large amounts of drag with some loss of lift. Spoilers have a similar but weaker effect and usually cause a slight nose-down change of trim as they are opened.

closing the airbrakes has only a limited effect and they can only be closed once. In the old days flying the T21b we used to say we were 'giving it a burst of no spoiler!'

It is the combination of the loss of lift and the increase in drag which makes even the simple 'spoilers' on the old T21b and Falke motor gliders an effective way of making the approach path more steep. With machines of a higher performance a much larger increase in drag is essential and more effective types are needed. These are sometimes known as 'dive' brakes as they are designed to be opened at any airspeed to limit the diving speed.

In most modern designs the airbrakes are speed limiting in a dive to an angle of 45° whereas earlier designs such as the Olympia, the Skylarks and the Capstan had airbrakes which would limit the speed to below VNE (the maximum diving speed allowed) in a continuous vertical dive. This is a useful feature if control is lost while flying in cloud as the pilot can open the airbrakes knowing that the speed will not become excessive. However, the modern requirements seem to be adequate although a little extra care is needed to avoid an unnecessarily high approach or excessive speed when landing in a small field.

Whereas it may have been acceptable for a low performance glider like the Tutor to have no airbrakes or spoilers so that the pilot had to rely on side-slipping for the approach control, a modern machine would become almost impossible to land accurately without good airbrakes. It is essential to be able to descend steeply over trees or other obstructions and to be able to control the glide path and float easily for an accurate spot landing. Without airbrakes the glide would be so flat and the float so far that landing accurately would be practically impossible.

Approach speeds

Although the airbrakes only raise the stalling speed by about 2–3 knots, it becomes necessary to increase speed for the approach by about 8–10 knots or risk a heavy landing. This is because of the effects of the extra drag caused by the airbrakes. As the round out is started there is a continuous loss of speed, and if the approach is started too slow there will not be sufficient speed or control left to round out and to prevent a bad landing. In other words the extra speed is required when the airbrakes are open to ensure a safe round out and a short float before touch down.

Each type of glider will need different minimum approach speeds for full airbrake and it is important to know what they are for the types you are flying. It is also important to learn to find time to glance at the ASI several times on every approach in order to check the actual speed. Never rely on judging the speed by attitude on the approach. Always check the actual speed on the ASI. Remember that a few knots extra will merely increase the float before touch down, whereas the loss of a few knots will result in, at best, a heavy landing.

Just after the final turn any loss of speed can be corrected by lowering the nose. However, if the speed gets too slow a little closer to the ground there will be neither the time nor the height to regain speed. A probable heavy landing can usually be averted by reducing the amount of airbrake. This both reduces the drag so that the speed is not lost rapidly and increases the lift so that the glider does not sink heavily on to the ground.

It is useful to know the minimum speeds which will allow a proper round out and hold-off for full airbrake, approximately half-airbrake, and no airbrake. These basic speeds will need to be increased in winds to allow for the extra losses caused by the wind shear (wind gradient and turbulence) near the ground.

On any approach where the speed becomes lower than this minimum speed for full airbrakes, the airbrake setting will have to be reduced to suit the speed – even if this means landing further into the field.

Simplifying the use of the airbrakes

There are various subtleties about the use of the airbrakes which need to be understood. As the airbrakes are opened the glider usually sinks rapidly five to ten feet before settling into the new glide path. You are liable to make a heavy, premature touch down if you open them too quickly near the ground. This sinking can be prevented by easing back on the stick as the airbrakes are opened and this technique must be mastered by the time that you are ready to start cross-country flying.

To avoid this problem, always try to arrange the final approach so that at least a half-airbrake is needed and has been applied for the final fifty feet or so. With most types of airbrake it is easiest to unlock them on the base leg so that there is no jerk when you open them. This is particularly helpful if you can see that the final turn is going to be rather low and that you will be inevitably opening the brakes close to the ground.

With very few exceptions, for example the K7, Skylark 2 and the American Schweitzer 134 and 232, it is practical to make the whole round out and touch down with full airbrake. If at first you find that full airbrake gives a worrying steep approach and high rate of descent, making the initial round-out height rather difficult to judge, the airbrakes can easily be closed a little. However, apart from landing the rather over-braked types mentioned, you should not get into the habit of reducing the amount of airbrake automatically on every landing in order to get a very smooth touch down. The landing should instead be made with the stick, moving it back gently as the glider begins to sink to obtain a good touch down, because any automatic reduction in the airbrake setting will make spot landings almost impossible.

The effects of airbrakes

There are several ways in which we can think of the effects of the airbrakes. Sometimes it is most useful to think of them as a means of throwing away excess height. Opening the brakes to get rid of two or three hundred feet is often safer than extending the downwind leg so that the final approach is very long.

On a very windy day, particularly on a hilltop site where a severe curl-over effect (downdraft) may occur, it is quite normal to make the final turn very high and close to the downwind boundary. The airbrakes are then used to throw away the excess height on the final approach. Because of the strong wind the approach will be very steep and any error in positioning the touch down will be too small to be important.

The airbrakes can be used at any stage of a flight to get rid of excess height in a controlled manner. Ideally, some excess height should be kept on the circuit at all times as a contingency against the risk of flying through an area of sinking air. This means that in most cases height will need to be lost on the base leg by using some airbrake. Once the excess height has been used up the airbrakes should be closed again, keeping them unlocked and ready for further use on the approach.

Another way of thinking of their effects is to consider them as the means of adjusting the gliding angle, particularly on the final approach.

Closing the airbrakes extends the glide and power pilots may like to think of their use as similar in principle to using the throttle. Moving the lever forward, like opening the throttle, will prevent an undershoot, but remember that their effect is only limited.

Airbrakes have a braking effect and always cause a loss of speed unless the nose of the glider is lowered the appropriate amount. When full airbrake is applied the nose *must* be lowered or within a few seconds there will be a loss of speed. However, caution is needed when reducing the amount of brake so as not to raise the nose. If an undershoot seems imminent it is better to allow the flying speed to build up to improve the penetration against the wind and to extend the float before touch down. If you attempt to keep the speed constant by raising the nose slightly as you close the airbrake you will nearly always find yourself a few seconds later at a critically low speed.

Occasionally while adjusting the approach to get down on to the landing area the speed may become excessive. This kind of situation may be rather deceptive since it may look as though the aircraft will only just reach the landing area. However, with the excess speed the float and hold-off will take the glider way down the field before it is ready to make a normal fully held-off landing. In a case like this you should open the airbrakes fully without lowering the nose so that the drag cuts down the excess speed and shortens the float.

But perhaps it is most important to think of reducing the airbrakes if the airspeed gets lower than the chosen speed and if there is insufficient height or time to lower the nose to regain it. Also, remember that if you are unhappy about the final approach or if it looks as though it will result in landing rather close to another machine or an obstruction, close those airbrakes and land in a clear area further ahead. Most gliders will float several hundred yards if the airbrakes are closed during the hold-off.

Finally, the airbrakes are there to use up height. Never use them before or during the final turn unless the turn itself will be higher than it really needs to be for an easy, safe approach. If the turn is rather low make sure that the airbrakes are closed and wait until that turn has been completed before you re-open them again.

6   Circuit planning

The aim in circuit planning is to bring the glider in to a position where it can complete the final turn at a safe enough height to make an easily controlled approach into the chosen landing area. However, the ideal position and height for this turn varies considerably from day to day because of the variations in the wind, the type of glider and the location of the field. Before flying cross-country the glider pilot needs to be able to weigh up all these factors for the field he has chosen to land in and this takes a considerable amount of experience and practice.

The final approach

The final approach needs to be long enough to allow time to assess how it is going and to make corrections to the glide path. The faster the approach speed, the longer the approach will need to be to allow time for these adjustments. This is the main reason that the final turn heights have increased since faster, more modern two-seaters have replaced the old T21 and, in the USA, the Schweizer 222 and 233; a lower approach simply does not give you time to put things right during the approach. It may not be hazardous on a calm day to complete the last turn at fifty feet, but it makes it very difficult to guarantee a spot landing.

In windy weather and particularly in the lee of hills where there may be severe downdrafts and turbulence, the final turn must be closer to the boundary of the field, but in normal conditions the turn really needs to be completed at least 275–365 metres (300–400 yards) behind the boundary of the landing area (about the length of an average farmer's field in most parts of the United Kingdom).

The easy way to get into this ideal position for the final turn is to make sure that you arrive opposite the landing area at about 500–600 feet. This ensures that you will not be embarrassed by being short of height and it enables you to sit out well to the side of the field giving you a fairly long base leg. To be sure of being able to complete the final turn in the correct position and at the correct height you need time on the base leg to assess whether you are rather high or low, or need to move further back or closer to the field. On a short base leg you may be able to see that things are going wrong but there is no time left to make an adjustment to put them right.

Weather conditions

The position for the turn on to the base leg is critical in windy weather since, with the very high ground speed flying downwind, even a few seconds' hesitation can put the base leg so far back that an undershoot may be inevitable. In windy conditions always turn early. It is then easy to allow the glider to drift back during the base leg until it is in an ideal position for the final turn.

During training and local soaring you are mainly concerned with landing back at the launch point or your gliding site, so you need to have a realistic idea of how much height you will lose flying from one end to the other. If the best gliding angle of your glider is reputed to be 25:1 in the state that you fly it, with dirt and dust on the wings and a little slip and skid here and there, it will probably glide about three and a half miles per 1,000 feet in smooth, still air. This means that on a calm day you need to allow almost 300 feet for each mile. If your winches are on the boundary and your field is 1,100 kilometres (1,200 yards) long you will usually use up about 200 feet on the downwind leg. However, remember that on a calm day you will need to put your base leg much further back than the downwind boundary and also that you may fly through some sink on the way. If the day is really calm you may only get 800 feet on your winch launch, in which case you may need luck to get back comfortably even if you turn on to the downwind leg immediately after release.

Height

If you are always slightly on the low side for the final parts of the circuit the problems multiply. You cannot sit well out to the side of the field and have a good base leg because, being short of height, you dare not put the final turn in an ideal position so that you have an adequate length of approach. The final turn will therefore be on the low side and you will find yourself landing hundreds of yards into the field – a long push back when training but a disaster on a cross-country flight.

The possibilities

Although we may aim at these ideal situations, from time to time they will not be achieveable and the essential thing is to recognise what is happening and to be able to deal with all the contingencies. This is far more important than learning to make circuits which are exactly square and which look nice to the instructor.

Most gliding operations have their own rules for local soaring and for circuit procedures. If you share your site with a power flying club these rules will be designed to separate the different kinds of traffic and make it easier for the power pilots to predict what you and your fellow gliders are going to do. This makes it a taboo to attempt to thermal below a certain height or on the circuit. Each site will be slightly different but there are points of general airmanship which should never normally be broken, whether the landing is at a gliding site or in a farmer's field at the end of a cross-country flight.

Therefore, once you have made the decision to make the landing, do not attempt to use any lift encountered. Always judge your height but monitor the Air Speed Indicator when flying below 500–600 feet and maintain your selected airspeed on the base leg, final turn and final approach. Never circle to use up height on or near the position for the base leg, or downwind of the landing area. Always choose a clear area for landing and never land directly in line with an obstruction, relying on a perfect landing or on the wheel brake to stop in time.

Joining the circuit

Rules for joining the circuit pattern vary from site to site. Some places have a rigid rule about entering the pattern over a particular landmark at a particular height. Others allow the pilot more freedom and discretion, suggesting that he should at least arrive opposite the landing area at an appropriate height. Good airmanship dictates that you settle down ready for the landing and make a reasonable base leg before the final turn.

Planning

The key to good circuit planning in the early stages is to be able to recognise a suitable position relative to the field by judging the angle. For example as you turn downwind to commence the circuit you should be glancing out sideways and downwards towards the nearest part of the field at an angle of 25–30°. Except in very low performance machines an angle of 45° is far too steep unless the conditions are very severe or it is clear that you are short of height for a normal circuit. It is always easier to be on a rather wide circuit moving closer than to be too close trying to move further out. This is because as you turn out to widen the circuit it becomes difficult to see the field and how far you have gone. It is a simple matter to learn to recognise what an angle of about 30° looks like. Pace out four paces from a mark on the ground and then just raise your arm and point to the mark. That is about the angle that you should need to see the nearest edge of the airfield or the landing area as you arrive opposite it at about 500–600 feet. However, this angle is only safe if you

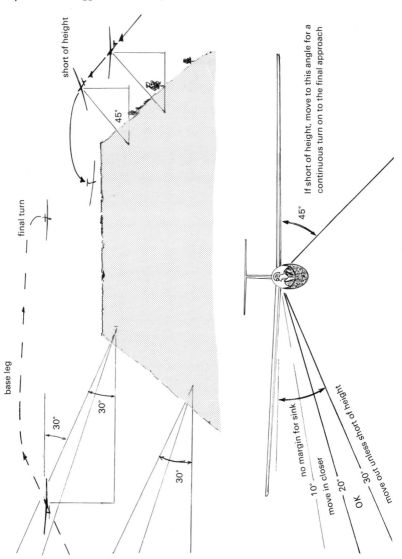

Positioning on the circuit by the angle down to the nearest part of the landing area.

have at least a normal amount of height. If you were higher than normal, say 700–800 feet you would be the appropriate distance further out, giving you a longer base leg and more time to make adjustments.

Angles

Angles alone are not safe because if you are very low the angle may be right but you will collide with the ground during the final turn. Unfortunately normal altimeters are notorious for sticking so that during the descent they may be misleading and indicate more than the true height. Combined with the human tendency to be optimistic, this kind of error leads to many hairy final turns and the occasional wrecked glider. At heights of over 500–600 feet an error of a couple of hundred feet will be relatively unimportant, provided that the angle is about right. Never trust the altimeter below that height and remember that, on any landing away from the gliding site, the ground level will almost always be different, making a further error possible.

Height

You may notice that I never actually mention the height for a final turn. This is because for me heights in feet do not exist below about 500 feet. I believe that, for training, the altimeter should be blanked off between 200 and 500 feet so that you just have to get into the habit of looking out to judge the final parts of the circuit and approach. Often in the past I have sneaked on an extra couple of hundred feet on the altimeter in a side-by-side two-seater after the pilot has declared to me that he never uses it. The result is usually a dramatically low final turn to the bewilderment of the pilot. Often the pilot quite genuinely believes that he ignores the instrument but his judgement is influenced by unconsciously reading it.

Speed and height

One other fundamental is worth noting here. If, during the circuit, you find yourself short of height, by the time you are down to about 500 feet it is vital to pick up some extra speed and maintain it from then on until the round out for landing. When flying downwind it is tempting to continue flying slowly to conserve height, but this can lead to situations in which an accident is almost unavoidable.

In order to make a safe final turn it is essential to have 10–12 knots above the minimum cruising speed. Below this speed the handling is usually too poor to allow safe turning in the turbulence near the ground. But it is only too easy to be misled into flying slowly in an attempt to conserve height. Looking down from the glider it seems obvious that you are not really short of height, but at low speed any encounter with turbulence or an area of sinking air will result in a serious loss of height. Within seconds this loss of height will put you in an impossible position. If you attempt a turn without increasing speed first you are liable to stall

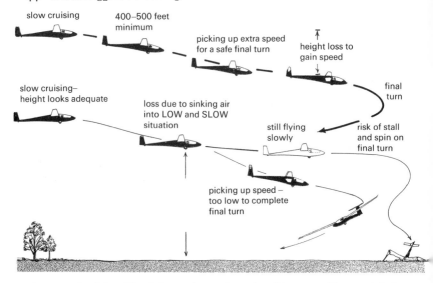

slow cruising

400–500 feet minimum

picking up extra speed for a safe final turn

height loss to gain speed

slow cruising– height looks adequate

final turn

loss due to sinking air into LOW and SLOW situation

still flying slowly

risk of stall and spin on final turn

picking up speed – too low to complete final turn

An example of the glider flying too low and too slow. Extra speed is essential when flying below 300–400 feet to be sure of a safe final turn.

and spin as a result of turning at too low an airspeed in turbulent air. Alternatively, if you attempt to gain more speed the height lost may leave you too low to complete the turn safely. This is the risk that you take any time you are flying low and slow, whether you are on the downwind or base leg of the circuit. Moreover, the risks are seldom obvious at the time because looking down from 200–300 feet there is still apparently plenty of height. Unfortunately quite a large amount of this height will inevitably be used up to gain speed for a safe final turn and this is easily forgotten in the anxiety of the moment. Combine this problem with a sticky altimeter and you can understand why so many people get caught making dangerously low and slow final turns.

To avoid the possibility of getting caught out like this, the first and most important thing is to acknowledge that you are running short of height and may have to turn in early or choose an alternative landing area. Plan for the worst situation that could happen. Where will you land if you hit further sink and lose more height? Get much closer to the field so that you do not have to waste height making a base leg. This is the time to fly within 45° of the boundary and to keep within that angle until you reach a landable area. Make a deliberate point of lowering the nose and picking up an appropriate speed, and keep checking the ASI every few seconds to make quite sure that you do not slow down again. Remember that if that happens, even for a few seconds, any patch of sink or turbulence could drop you into a position where you are low and slow and in real trouble. Ignore the altimeter and try to judge whether you can continue to fly downwind further or should be making the final turn. Compare your height with any trees or buildings, judging the situation by rememberng that you probably want to complete that final turn by at least two or three times their height.

Usually you will be making a 180° turn in this situation and it will obviously use up more height than the normal turn of 90° from a base leg to the final approach. Since you will be turning in over the field instead of some distance behind it, you will want to get rid of height very quickly after completing the turn. Be ready to check the airspeed as you are completing the turn and, it if is adequate, open full airbrake immediately to get rid of the excess height. Then, if there is still plenty of room left for the landing, you can reduce the amount of airbrake if you need to because of a high rate of sink or loss of airspeed.

7 Circuit planning in special conditions

Sites

It would be impossible to cover all the special conditions which have to be taken into account at different gliding sites. Each has its own peculiarities and traps for the unwary which need to be understood by those flying there. However, it is important to realise that in a different location procedures designed to cater for a particular hazard on one site may themselves create a problem elsewhere. Thus, while the effects of a strong curl-over in the lee of a ridge of hills may necessitate keeping very close to the field on the base leg to avoid the risk of an undershoot, the same positioning on a field landing in open country would almost certainly result in a dangerous overshoot.

It is important therefore not only to learn how to get down safely and accurately on your own site, but to understand any special circumstances which apply there. Experience of flying at other sites is invaluable because of the need to recognise the special circumstances and to modify your planning accordingly. However, it is important to realise that it is only on the first circuit and landing that you make in a new place, or on the first flight of the day at your home site, that you use your judgement. On subsequent flights you simply compare your positioning with that of the first flight. So on your first flight you should make a special point of landing accurately on a chosen spot to test your judgement and ability. Then if you land several hundred yards further on it is conclusive proof that you cannot yet rely on your judgement or flying for an accurate landing. It is no good thinking or claiming that you could have landed on the spot if you had really wanted to. You didn't make it and you are not yet as competent as you should be.

Heights

With a car or winch launch the need to think and plan the circuit quickly becomes apparent. The pilot is often faced with unavoidable problems such as cable breaks or abnormally low launches when it becomes impossible to join the circuit at a pre-determined height. But no matter what type of launch is being used it is still vital to have experience of planning from various positions and heights.

It is always easiest to start the circuit with a downwind leg and with sufficient height to guarantee being opposite the landing area with at least 500 feet. Running short of height is an embarrassment but it is equally ridiculous to start the downwind leg with so much height that you arrive back at this position at more than 700 or 800 feet. Normally

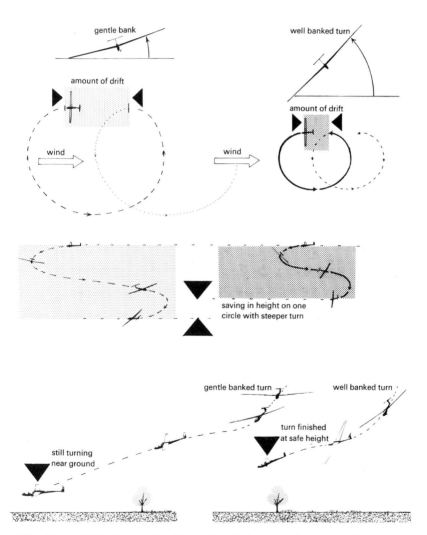

The effects of drift when circling. Use well banked turns so that you lose less height and reduce the distance the glider drifts with the wind.

you would be searching for thermals, practising turns and so on with any spare height, and it is just a matter of turning on to the downwind leg at a suitable height. Whenever possible you should practise flying and searching for lift upwind and to the side of the field. If a thermal is found this enables you to climb a considerable way before having to give up because of drifting too far downwind of the field.

Perhaps you have a little too much height and are thinking about doing a 360° turn to use it up. Although a well banked turn will normally use up 50–100 feet, if you happen to turn into an area of sink this may easily be 200 feet or more. This is most likely to be the case when you hit an obviously strong bit of lift and try to use it. As you start the turn you fall into that very strong sink close by and within seconds you are several hundred feet worse off. This means that you should always ask yourself before you make a 360° turn, 'Can I afford to lose 200 feet and drift back?' If this would leave you in a difficult or marginal position, do not circle. Think of some other way to use up the height, such as widening the circuit or even using the airbrakes. Above all, if you do decide to circle make it a well banked turn. This will reduce the amount of time you spend in the turn and minimise the height lost if you fly into sink.

Provided that you are not being forced to drift away from the field by a cross-wind, it is perfectly all right to turn away from the field, and the choice of turning right or left should depend on your position at the time. If you are already rather close and are looking down at a steep angle, turn out and away to improve your positioning slightly. At every stage of the flight try to improve your positioning first and then worry about getting rid of any excess height. If you are obviously too high and too close, move away to improve your position first and then, if you are still too high, use up the remaining height. If you try to use up the height first by circling you will find that you are still positioned badly and have a problem getting into an ideal position for your approach.

Most beginners tend to fly on a converging course to the field as they fly back downwind. Make a point of checking and re-checking that you are not converging and that the angle between you and the nearest landing area is still about 30°, unless you think you are running short of height. If the angle is getting too steep, make a definite, well banked turn and steer off to improve the position as soon as you can. A gentle, gradual turn will not help much and you will find you are still too close by the time you have to turn on to the base leg.

Landings

Somewhere along the downwind leg, depending on the site, the weather and various other factors such as the whims of your instructor, you must prepare for the landing. There are several recognised pre-landing checks but the most vital items to remember are to put the wheel down, if it is retractable, to pick up speed and re-trim, to put your hand on the airbrakes ready to use them and to disregard the altimeter from then on. Whatever happens these things must be done by about 500 feet, and from then on the important things are to judge the heights for the rest of the circuit and to keep monitoring the ASI and maintaining your chosen speed. Make sure that you have looked for and seen any other traffic on the circuit, have checked that the wind has not changed and that you have a clear landing area available.

The last part of the downwind leg, the base leg and the final approach are the busiest times of all for the pilot. Concentrating too much on any one item will result in something going wrong. The art is to keep checking everything continuously as in the following imaginary reconstruction of what goes on in a pilot's head.

Going downwind – speed OK? Angle to the nearest landing area OK? 'Looks a bit close, turn out quickly'. Landing area clear? 'No, one glider on the right-hand edge, but I can land well clear of it on the left'. Wind sock? 'Still the same slight cross-wind from the left'. Height OK? 'Plenty, going to be a little high, but the angle is about right now.' Speed up to 55 knots and re-trimmed. Other traffic? 'Nothing near, K8 just launching'. Hand on brakes and last glance at altimeter. 'Says 600 feet so probably about 500, so height OK.' Angle about right? Speed still OK? 'Angle looks OK but speed down to 50 knots, lower the nose a little'. Light wind so position of the turn on to base needs to be just after the boundary of the landing area passes the wing-tip; turning now. 'Angle looks steep, stop the turn early to move back further.' Speed? 'Does it look as though I will be much too high for the final turn?' 'Move back a little more and open the airbrakes to get down a bit, speed down to 50 again. Low enough now so close the brakes again.' 'When should I start the final turn?' 'Start banking now, well banked turn, speed 55.' 'Will I need the airbrakes on as soon as the turn is finished?' 'Yes, still rather high so full brake immediately, speed 52, nose down a little.'

Trying to write all these thoughts down makes one realise what a very heavy work-load the pilot has on a normal approach and landing. If you can manage to be thinking one stage ahead all the time, it can all be kept under control. But once you get behind all you can do is to try to extricate yourself from the awkward situations which will keep occuring and to clear up the mess as best you can.

Making your own decisions

Although at first you need guidance and help with the planning, after a few circuits and a comprehensive briefing you will learn very little if your instructor keeps on telling you 'Turn on to the base leg now' or

'Open the airbrakes now' and so on. You need to be left to make your own decisions as far as is practical and safe. Often the instructor can help by suggesting to you what you ought to be thinking, saying something like 'Remember, if you think you are much higher than you need to be, either use up the height with the airbrakes or move further back. You decide' or 'Think ahead during this final turn so that you can decide when and how much airbrake you will need on the approach. I'll leave it up to you.'

If the conditions are unstable, areas of lift and sink will upset your planning so that you may have to change your plans quickly to prevent things getting right out of hand. Ideally, you need to experience dealing with awkward situations rather than just practising 'perfect' circuits in

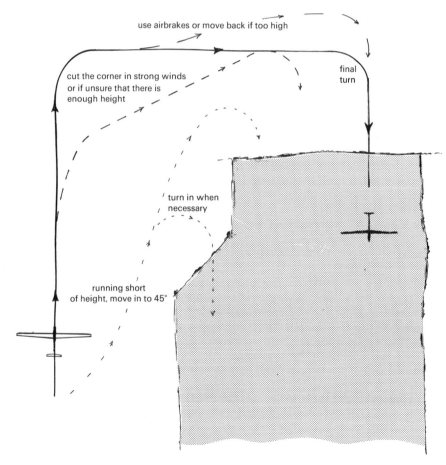

use airbrakes or move back if too high

final turn

cut the corner in strong winds
or if unsure that there is
enough height

turn in when
necessary

running short
of height, move in to 45°

Variations on the base leg.

stable conditions. In addition to experience of running out of height, it is important to learn to join the circuit after soaring flights where you may have gained little or no height yet have drifted back behind the landing area. This is likely to happen on early soaring flights from a car or winch launch, and often leads to dangerously bad planning if you haven't done it several times before. If the height permits always try to work back upwind and join the circuit normally. When less height is available try to move well out to one side of the landing area first so that at least you will have a good base leg to adjust your height and position. But never start to circle to try to use a thermal or to use up height on or near the downwind boundary. If you hit sink and drift back when circling you can easily find yourself unable to get back against the wind to the landing area. Remember that on many occasions you may be operating in a cross-wind so that the downwind boundary will be on one side of the field. In this case circling on the downwind side to use up height or to try to use lift is dangerous.

If you are already established in lift and drift back it is relatively safe to continue as long as you are still within easy gliding reach of the field. But always allow for the possibility of meeting sinking air as well as having the head wind to contend with. Until you are experienced and are flying gliders with a good performance, an angle of about 30° is a sensible limit. Avoid flying over the landing area. This is an awkward position to escape from because as you fly away from it you cannot see how far you have flown. If the height permits fly well off to the side to give you a long base leg. This will give you time to reposition yourself for the final turn and to use up any excess height with the airbrakes on the base leg.

Using the airbrakes

There is nothing fundamentally against using the airbrakes in the final turn, provided that the speed is monitored frequently and maintained and, of course, provided that there will be still more height than is necessary to be able to complete the turn by a safe height. However, it is probably wise for the inexperienced pilot to avoid suddenly opening the airbrakes during the turn unless he is ridiculously high. Opening the airbrakes will cause a loss of speed unless the nose is lowered the appropriate amount, and if this is not done it will only take a few seconds to lose enough speed to be critically near to stalling – a very serious situation on the final turn. Therefore unless the height is really excessive it is advisable to finish the turn first before opening the brakes fully to use up that height. If, on the other hand, you are on the base leg with the airbrakes already out and it is clear that the turn will still be very high, provided that you are careful to monitor the airspeed and maintain it during the turn, it would be reasonable to continue the turn with the airbrakes out. But watch out. The rate of descent will be very high so you need to be ready to close the airbrakes if you find you have used up your excess.

Never use the airbrakes before or during a final turn unless you can see that otherwise you will have excess height by the time you have completed it. Many narrow escapes and dangerously low final turns occur because the pilot automatically opens the brakes without considering how high the turn will be completed. Always try to compare your height with nearby trees or buildings so that you are not misled into using the airbrakes because your angle to the landing area looks steep. Remember that a steep angle could mean either that you are too high or that you are far to close to the landing area. Make sure that you can always finish the final turn at a safe height. If it looks a little on the low side, close the brakes immediately until the turn has been completed.

Learning by your mistakes

In some ways flying from a large gliding site is a disadvantage during basic training because the seriousness of poor planning is not always apparent. Running short of height simply means turning in to land further up the field and a longer push back for the next launch. This would never do on a field landing where a poorly planned approach might result, at best, in a badly damaged glider. Therefore, it is normally a bad habit to gamble by trying to soar in lift low down and to rely on not meeting any sink on the way back downwind.

In reality every circuit should be made with sufficient reserve of height to ensure that an area of sink cannot seriously upset the planning or positioning for a good approach. Somewhere on the base leg this reserve of height must be reduced by using the airbrakes so that by the final turn the height and position allow an accurate and controllable approach. Obviously, any approach with little or no airbrake is dangerously low. However, any approach requiring full airbrake continuously is dangerously high except in very windy weather, since it results in an overshoot if any lift is encountered on the approach.

Side-slipping

When landing in a restricted area at any time that full airbrake is required for more than a few seconds, it would be wise to start side-slipping. This will usually get you down quickly to a position where less than full airbrake is needed so that the situation is once more under control. Every cross-country pilot should be capable of making safe and accurate full airbrake side-slips for this purpose. It is little use being able to get into a side-slip of sorts after a delay of some seconds while you think about which rudder you will need. Side-slip approaches need to be practised regularly. On almost every approach I make in a solo glider on my home site, I do a few seconds of side-slipping so that I never get out of practice. This does not mean slipping near the ground. The side-slip should only be necessary to get rid of any excess height that is beyond the power of the airbrakes, and it should be apparent when you need to do it shortly after opening the brakes, high up on the approach. Side-slipping close to the ground is a sign of poor planning and should never be necessary.

Beginners have to accept overshooting the ideal touch-down point when they arrive too close or too high. They should not attempt to side-slip until they have been taught to do it and have practised it with an instructor a number of times.

8 Directional control on the ground

Design considerations

Many pilots have commented on the difficulty they have experienced during take-off and landing in modern gliders. There have been numerous cases of serious swings, ground loops and wing-tips digging into the ground which have tended to give some of them a reputation for being tricky.

Whereas most of the earlier designs had a substantial front skid and the wheel mounted slightly behind the centre of gravity (c.g.) the modern trend has been to move the wheel well forward and so do away with the front skid and the need for a heavy keel structure. This arrangement has many advantages, but two major problems: one, the excessive tail loads during ground handling, and the other the added difficulty in getting good directional control on the ground. Whereas a small ground trolley solves the ground-handling problem, we have to learn to live with the new swinging characteristics if we want simple retracting undercarriages and lightweight gliders.

The newer arrangement is very similar in dynamics to a tail-wheel light aircraft. Once a swing has started the mass of the aircraft being centred behind the wheel accentuates the swing, and a ground loop can occur. This is particularly likely to occur in calm conditions when the glider is rolling quite fast and is on a smooth surface so that the tail skid can slip sideways more easily. This is in contrast to the arrangement when the c.g. is ahead of the wheel, helping to damp out the swing like a modern tricycle undercarriage.

Furthermore, when the wheel is further forward there is a greater tendency for the aircraft to swing into the wind on the ground because the extra side area behind the wheel increases the weathercocking tendency. This means that directional control in a cross-wind, that is the power of the rudder to prevent the glider weathercocking into wind while it is on the ground, is considerably less on the modern machines. In the air, the rudder control on all these types seems quite adequate.

It has been suggested that the use of a towing hook mounted well back in a position suitable for winch launching is a disadvantage for aerotowing in cross-winds because the tow rope loads do little to help pull the glider straight. (The problems of swinging on take-off are worse when the acceleration is poor as on aerotowing.) Obviously a nose hook would

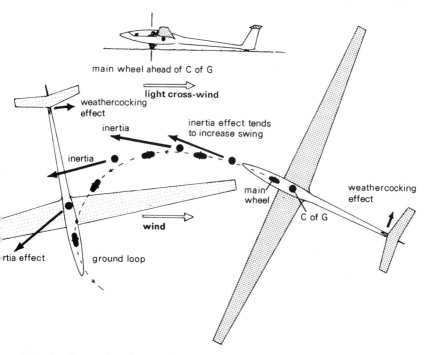

Directional control on the ground.

be of some benefit, but once the glider is moving the tow rope loads are not very high and a very serious swing must occur before the pull of the tow rope would be at a sufficient angle to influence things much. At flying speeds the rope loads are only about 22.5kg (50lb). However, in a strong cross-wind this effect can be taken advantage of by positioning the glider slightly to the upwind side of the tug so that this side load is available at the start of the take-off run when the rope loads are very much higher.

Problems with control

We know from experience that modern gliders can be operated in very severe cross-winds and that the effectiveness of their ailerons is little different from the previous generation of machines. Why, then, do so many pilots have difficulty?

One of the main reasons, it would seem from observing pilots taking off in cross-winds, is a reluctance to anticipate what may happen by starting with full rudder applied. If we start with no rudder and apply it as soon as the slightest swing has started, this swing will be into wind and only a limited rudder power will be available to stop it. However, if we start with full rudder applied, even if it is too much and causes a swing out of wind this is far less critical and is easily stopped by a reduction in the movement.

Similarly, with keeping the wings level it is important not to get into a position where the into-wind wing is up or at low speeds the aileron control will be marginal in preventing a wing-tip touching the ground. Unfortunately in all flying except cross-wind take-offs and landings and side-slipping, we are conditioned into co-ordinating stick and rudder and into steering by means of banked turns. If we observe inexperienced pilots landing it is common to see them attempting to steer on the ground by using bank, and this is the usual reason for the wing-tip to touch the ground prematurely. By the time that the pilot realises that the glider is banked, the speed is too low for effective control. It is a vital part of training to teach steering on the ground and to ensure that the pilot is using the right technique, or he will be unable to avoid collisions on the ground and will have difficulties in cross-winds. This is by no means obvious to a pilot under training, and since occasions for steering on the ground are usually few and far between, it is easy to assume that he is doing the right thing.

Most experienced pilots consider that they have this all buttoned up, but on the few occasions when they have a completely unexpected swing they are quite likely – having applied full rudder – to help it with aileron. A few seconds later if the rudder does take effect the yawing movement causes a rapid rolling and the wing-tip is on the ground.

On a car or winch launch, provided that there is a completely clear space available, the swinging is relatively unimportant and can be held with the rudder. However, if the pilot prefers he can release, in which case the glider will run into wind. Special care should be taken to avoid a swing starting in light winds. It is keeping the wings level or the into-wind wing down in a cross-wind which is the vital part.

How to improve control

All this adds up to the need for more anticipation on the part of the pilots and the need for special care to allow enough room at the launch point for the occasional swing or ground loop to happen without the glider running into another parked aircraft or obstruction. From time to time this will happen, and considerably more frequently than with the earlier breeds of glider, so that it just is not good enough to rely on piloting skill to avoid what could be a very expensive accident.

If we apply the same kind of argument to cross-wind landing techniques it will be seen that it is better to touch down with an overcorrection of the drift than to fail to correct enough. This is particularly so with the 'wheel well forward' set-up when touching down with drift due to the cross-wind – particularly in light winds – which can easily lead to the start of a possible ground loop.

It looks as though while wheels will stay in their present position, fuselages are still getting slimmer and wing-tips lower. All these factors plus the general trend towards heavier machines make control on the ground at low speed more critical.

9 Learning to aerotow

The great advantage of aerotowing compared with any other form of launching is that you can release at whatever height you like (or can afford). Also you can be towed around to cover a large area so that you can almost always release at a favourable moment when you are in lift. It is possible to operate from a relatively narrow strip of moderate length compared with the length of run required to have satisfactory launches with a winch or tow car. Unfortunately this requires a fair degree of skill from the pilot so that an absolute beginner must accept that on an early flight the launch is one of the parts of the flight that he won't be able to do.

The take-off

At the start of the take-off run the key things are to keep the wings level and to stay directly behind the tug. Keeping the wings level will require large movements of the ailerons at first because the low speed means poor control. Normally the tow rope will help to keep the glider straight but inevitably some swing may occur and need correction. Of course the swing may be in either direction and at the same time either wing may drop. So both the stick and the rudder have to be used quite independently while the aircraft is on the ground. With both controls you will probably need a large correction to stop the swing or wing drop followed by a quick reduction of movement once it is taking effect, or you will end up with a wing on the ground. Always be ready to grab the release knob to release the rope if a wing drops and you are unable to pick it up off the ground almost immediately. Since the take-off and landing runs are so short it is difficult to get much practice at steering on the ground – a vital part of learning to glide. Therefore, it is useful experience to deliberately steer off to one side or the other after landing just for the practice.

During the take-off it is important to get the glider up on to the main wheel as soon as possible to reduce the ground resistance. With the older machines such as the K7 and K13, and ones fitted with a nose wheel like the K21 and Grob 103, this is a matter of easing back on the stick to lift the nose off. Since the main wheel is ahead of the centre of gravity on gliders such as the K6 and K18, and most of the aircraft have a retractable wheel, this will mean moving well forward on the stick to get the tail off the ground. A small backward movement may be necessary to help the glider unstick but do not try to pull it off the ground before it is ready to fly.

The climb

Because the tow plane is accelerating all the time the glider will tend to climb once it has left the ground. To stay in position without climbing the glider has to be flown more and more nose-down. Do not try to keep too close to the ground. Try to keep about four or five feet up, say level with the top of the tug, and watch the tug and not the ground in front of you. If you try to keep very low you will often start to oscillate and perhaps even fly into the ground heavily. This is far less likely to happen if you fly a little higher. Watch the tug and try to fly steadily, keeping the wings level in the normal way using stick and rudder together. In particular, if a wing drops pick it up immediately with a firm movement of the stick and rudder.

Once the tow plane has left the ground it may either start to climb away immediately, gathering climbing speed as it goes, or it may be held down flying level to gain speed. As the tow plane starts to climb you will need to nose up to follow it or you will be left in the turbulent wake. If this happens you will probably have difficulty in keeping the wings level as the wake will buffet you and tend to make one of the wings drop. Be very careful as you move up into a normal towing position. Moving up too quickly and so getting too high during the initial climb is the most likely cause of the very serious towing accidents where the tug aircraft is pulled out of control into a vertical dive by the glider.

Contrary to popular opinion this problem is almost certainly initiated by the glider pilot keeping too close to the ground just after take-off. As the tug climbs away, accelerating upwards rapidly because of moving up through the wind gradient, the glider pilot suddenly finds himself far too low and in the wake. Then as he in turn moves up through the gradient, his seemingly small movement on the stick results in a very rapid zoom up into a position which is far too high for safe towing. This can be further exaggerated by towing on a release hook which is close to the c.g., especially if the glider is being flown by a light pilot so that the normal stability is reduced. So watch the tug and not the ground and do not get left too low as he starts to climb. Above all, make any movement upwards in small steps instead of trying to move all the way in one go.

Positioning

The exact towing position is not very critical – it is the rapid changes which are dangerous. Some instructors still teach keeping the towing

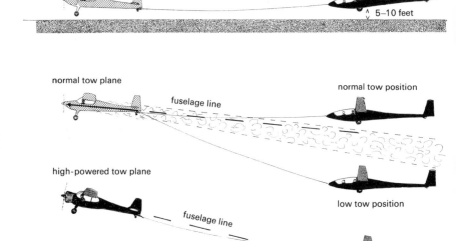

on take off – do not climb

5–10 feet

normal tow plane

fuselage line

normal tow position

normal tow position

low tow position

high-powered tow plane

fuselage line

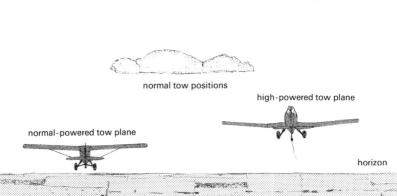

normal tow positions

high-powered tow plane

normal-powered tow plane

horizon

Aerotowing. The normal tow position is just above the extended fuselage line and just clear of the turbulent wake.

aircraft in a certain position in relation to the horizon, but this is not ideal because it is quite impossible to do this on those occasions when the horizon is completely obscured or you are flying in hilly country. Also, the position of the tug in relation to the horizon varies considerably, depending on the power of the tug. Thus, one type of tug will be well above the horizon while another which does not climb so steeply will be a little below.

Many tow planes have a paint line from nose to tail down the fuselage.

The glider will be well clear of the wake as long as it is not below the extension of that line. Often it is easy to note the exact position of the tow plane by looking at the wing or the top of the fin in relation to the cabin, and by maintaining the same view of the tow plane you will stay in position. Once you have established a suitable position another way is to note the exact relationship between the nose of the glider and the towing aircraft and to keep this constant. This method is particularly suitable when the glider has a long nose so that the position of the tug can be sighted against it more easily. By keeping the tug in the same place on the canopy and moving it back into position each time it varies, it is very easy to hold station. Most experienced pilots are not really aware of how to keep their positioning and they probably use a combination of all these methods.

Problems for beginners

Holding position is often a problem for the beginner and it is best to make a number of flights before attempting the tow. By then the co-ordination of the stick and rudder will be well established which will make keeping in position much easier. It is true to say that if you could keep the glider's wings parallel with those of the tug you would stay in position, but it is a mistake to think that then you only need the rudder to keep lined up. Try to use the normal co-ordination of stick and rudder all the time on tow. Using the rudder alone to keep behind the tug at best creates a lot of drag and, with those types of glider which have weak lateral stability, simply does not work.

Elevator movements

Because of the relatively high towing speed the elevator will be super-sensitive. Ideally you should make tiny corrections to prevent the glider from getting out of position. Always move up or down very slowly and in small steps rather than attempt to get back to the correct position in one movement. Make a tiny control movement in the direction you need to go and then check it with a counter-move.

If you try to move down quickly the glider will gain speed and tend to overtake the tug, making a bow in the rope. If this becomes tight with a big jerk it will cause a nose-up pitching movement and you will usually arrive back too high with more slack in the rope. If a very bad bow occurs it is probably best to release the rope rather than break it a few seconds later. However, with experience the shock of jerking the rope tight can be relieved by lowering the glider's nose just as the rope is tightening. This speeds up the glider, preventing the snatch. Usually this will necessitate going down into the wake for a few moments, but it does save the rope.

If the glider gets too low it is important to move up slowly. Moving up puts an extra load on the rope and therefore it is unwise to make any movement upwards if there is about to be a jerk from a slack rope. The combination of the jerk and pulling up is the most common time to break a rope.

All these problems are eliminated by holding the position accurately and avoiding large elevator movements. Remember: do not overcontrol.

Keeping in line

Keeping in line with the tow plane is largely a matter of responding very quickly whenever a wing drops. Unlike the elevator control, which is usually much more sensitive than at gliding speeds, the main effect on the ailerons is that they become very much heavier. Try to sense when a wing drops and apply a firm movement of the stick and rudder together to bring the wings level quickly. Unless you make the correction very quickly you will find your glider moving out to the side. If you are still learning to tow do not try to get back behind the tow plane. Just bring the wings level, or to the same angle of bank as the tug ahead if it is in a turn. If you try to get back into line straight away you will overshoot the position and start to swing from side to side. Just bringing the wings level will stop any swinging and you will find the glider gradually being pulled back into line.

Handling

The handling necessary to fly back into line quickly is not simple. It involves initiating a small turn towards the tug and then reversing the turn neatly as the correct position is reached. Until you can manage the whole tow unaided you will find it easier just to bring the wings level and let the glider do the rest.

During the tow the tug pilot is responsible for the look out and until you are experienced you should concentrate on positioning and keeping your eyes on the tug. For training purposes it is usual to tow up to a definite height, so a very quick glance at the altimeter is necessary from time to time. As you come up to the release height always have a quick look round to make quite sure that you will be clear to turn off after releasing the rope. Glance down to identify the release knob, pull it twice hard, watch the rope and make sure it has gone and then pull up into a climbing turn in the direction you have chosen. In the UK the turn may be made in either direction. Never put an extra load on the rope before you release and never start your pull-up and turn before you have seen that the rope has gone. Otherwise you will stand the tow plane on its nose if the release fails to operate or if you pull the wrong knob by mistake.

Immediately after release it is wise to check your position in relation to the gliding site. Your ears have become accustomed to the much higher towing speed and anything much slower will sound and feel dangerously slow. Make a point of slowing right down almost to a stall before re-trimming to your cruising speed or you will find yourself continuing to fly far too fast and unable to soar.

Release in lift

In soaring conditions it is almost always better to release in lift rather than to tow up to a set height and find yourself in sink. About 300 feet below your chosen launch height be ready to release as soon as the variometer shows an abnormally high rate of climb indicating that you are in good lift. Even then you will probably have to backtrack to re-find the lift. At towing speeds the variometer lag and the distance taken to turn after release will usually have taken you well past the area of lift. Never wait for the best indication before getting off tow.

As a general rule, check that the rope has gone and then pull up into a tight turn, straightening up a little after you have turned through 180° or so. After a few seconds you should be back into the area of lift you meant to release in. If you do not release in lift the chances are that you will find yourself in sink, wasting hundreds of feet searching for anything which will keep you up.

10 Winch and car launching emergencies

In spite of all the briefings and practice at dealing with cable breaks and launch failures, it is clear from the accident statistics that many pilots are at risk when making car or winch launches. The trouble is that we all tend to believe we are ready and able to deal with any eventuality. Unfortunately unless we keep in regular practice both our decision making and our flying tends to deteriorate.

Cable breaks

As a pilot gains in solo experience the possibility of a cable break becomes less of a worry so that the way in which it is dealt with is likely to be less methodical than before. If good habits have been established during training the same habits will stand the pilot in good stead throughout his flying career.

Unfortunately a few poorly chosen words repeated again and again by the instructor can produce a habit which, in the excitement and anxiety of an unexpected launch failure, may prove fatal. For example the words 'stick hard forward' in response to a cable break can be very dangerous if the break occurs just after leaving the ground. It can easily result in flying into the ground in a steep dive before the pilot has time to make a further movement. This has caused a number of accidents in the past. Near the ground it is important to level out any climb immediately and, if the height allows, to put the aircraft into a normal glide.

On no account should the airbrakes be used unless the ASI has been read and indicates that the speed is adequate. If the initial climb happens to be rather slow at the moment of failure the glider may be almost down to the stalling speed by the time that the nose has been lowered into the glide. Then, even though it is obvious from the noise that the speed is increasing, there will still be far too little speed for anything but a no-brake landing. So the golden rule is never to use the airbrakes unless you have had time to read the ASI and have confirmed that you have sufficient speed (usually a minimum of about 50 knots for most machines).

When a break occurs near the ground there will always be plenty of room ahead, so let the glider float on. Remember that with no airbrake the speed will diminish very slowly so that the hold-off will have to be very gentle to avoid ballooning. When the wheel eventually touches the

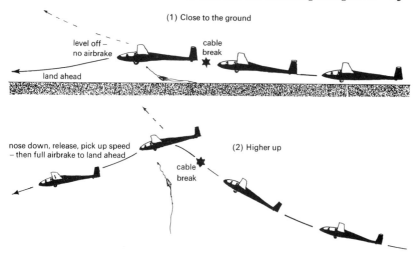

(1) Close to the ground

level off –
no airbrake

cable
break

land ahead

nose down, release, pick up speed
– then full airbrake to land ahead

cable
break

(2) Higher up

If you have a cable break near the ground, level out, release the cable end and land without airbrake. If you have a cable break higher up, keep the nose down and release the cable end, pick up speed and, if there is room to land ahead, check the speed and then use the airbrakes.

ground, open the airbrakes immediately. This will stop any tendency for the glider to leave the ground again and will also shorten the ground run.

Dealing with other mechanical failures

Whereas an actual cable break may be fairly obvious, a gradual mechanical failure such as is caused by fuel starvation or a puncture on the tow car will take longer to detect. If one of these kinds of failure happens just after leaving the ground only very quick reactions can prevent a 'nasty'. Always be ready for the possibility of a failure during the first part of the launch and if the acceleration fades, assume the worst. Don't hold on hopefully. Lower the nose and release at once. Then make sure that you check the airspeed before you open the airbrakes.

The effects of height and speed

It is important to realise that cable break procedures cannot be safely determined by the height at which the break occurs. If the glider happens to be flying at a very low speed because of a slow reaction or a rather slow launch, the indicated height might seem plenty for a quick 360°

turn. However, starting the turn without regaining a sensible airspeed first would certainly add your name to the accident sheet. By the time you regained 50 to 55 knots (the speed that you need for a safe turn) the situation would probably look very different and the safe decision might well be to go straight ahead.

Much depends on the wind strength and the speed of the launch. Whereas a slow launch on a calm day will result in a very long ground run so that landing ahead may be marginal from quite a low break, on a windy day a landing ahead will very often be possible from a height which is ample for a full circuit.

Marginal situations

In a marginal situation on a small site the time taken to look at the altimeter and to think about the reading may make the difference between an easy and a difficult decision. For example if you set yourself x hundred feet as the minimum for a full circle and on looking at the altimeter find it reads a little lower, any delay may put you in a position from which a circuit is dangerous and anything else very marginal.

It is always a wise move to think carefully about the best course of action to take for a launch failure before you take off. On a small site this is vital. However, it is usually only after lowering the nose and releasing the cable that the situation can be properly assessed. Even when practising simulated cable breaks it is seldom possible to predict what will be the right action to take until after the nose has been lowered. If you try to rely on pre-made decisions or, as some instructors recommend, call out your choice as you go up each launch, you may still find an unexpected situation when you look ahead after a cable break. There is also the risk that you may forget to carry out this routine as you get more experienced so that when an actual break occurs you do not have a systematic way of dealing with it. I believe that it may be safer in the long run to learn to use the same routine method of decision making.

First reactions

The first reaction to any kind of launch failure should be to lower the nose to regain flying speed and to pull the release knob twice hard. (When the height allows, lower the nose into an 'approach' attitude to pick up at least 50 knots.) Then look ahead and ask yourself 'Can I land in the space ahead?' If the answer is 'yes', check the ASI reading and if, and only if, it is adequate, open the airbrakes. Whenever possible open full airbrake at first to use up the excess height quickly. Then if there is plenty of room ahead the setting can be reduced for the final stages of the approach when the rate of sink is very high or the speed begins to decay.

If you have the slightest doubt about getting down safely into the space available, or if that is clearly impossible, check that the speed is still adequate and turn off with a well banked turn. The direction of this turn should have been pre-determined before take-off but if this has not been done, don't dither, turn off anyway. Then decide whether there is room to turn back into wind and land ahead or whether that is difficult or doubtful. In the latter case keep turning with a well banked turn, monitoring the airspeed and the angle of bank. If height permits the turn can be stopped to straighten up downwind for a few seconds before completing the turn and making an approach into wind.

Summary of first reactions

Put the nose down, release the cable, look ahead. Ask yourself 'Can I land ahead?' If so, check the speed. Apply full airbrake and make a slight turn to the best area ahead. If you cannot get down in the space ahead or are doubtful, check the speed and turn off with a well banked turn. Look and decide whether it is easiest to turn back into wind (usually known as an S-turn) or to make a full circle. Check the bank and airspeed during the turns and be ready to apply the airbrake for the final approach. If height allows, extend the circle with a short downwind leg but be careful not to run yourself short of height.

Timing your reactions

Experience shows that either reacting quickly and decisively or being slow to react can create dangerous situations. An unpremeditated, quick 360° turn seems to be a common cause of many stall and spin accidents. Indecision can also lead to getting into unredeemable situations.

Notice that the decision to make an S-turn or a full circle does not have to be made initially. However, it is important not to dither while facing into wind as the amount of room ahead decreases rapidly together with the loss of height, making the decisions more difficult or even impossible. Remember, if you cannot get down ahead or have the slightest doubts about doing so, turn off without delay. Then decide on the safest plan of action. When possible check your actual height by comparing it with the height of any nearby trees or tall buildings.

Low turns

If you elect to make a continuous turn keep rechecking your airspeed (50 knots minimum, more in rough conditions) and make sure that you maintain a well banked turn. It is important to realise that if you have allowed the nose to drop and the speed to increase during the turn because of excess bank, there is never any need to allow the glider to fly into the ground. Low turns tend to have a hypnotic effect on an inexperienced pilot and spiralling down and flying into the ground at high speed is not unknown. If the speed and the angle of bank have become rather excessive the turn can always be completed by reducing the angle of bank and pulling back so that no more height is lost. Most gliders will be able to turn at least 180° with no loss of height if the speed at the start of the turn is 60 knots or more.

Of course the cable may break or the launch fail at any height so that a 360° turn can often be stopped half-way to fly a little way downwind before turning into wind for the final approach. But do not set your heart on getting back to the normal landing area. Maintain your approach speed as you fly downwind and judge the moment to turn in by comparing your height and not by looking at the altimeter. Make the turn before you think you are getting too low for comfort.

A common cause of dangerously low turns in these situations is for the pilot to decide on the position for the final turn beforehand and to try to get there even though the height becomes marginal. Above all if you do end up a little lower than you intended, make sure that you maintain speed and use plenty of bank for the turn. Don't over-rudder and whatever you do don't let the glider fly into the ground. If necessary, straighten up and land out of wind if there is room. Having completed

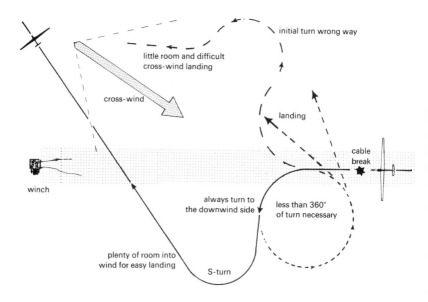

S-turn cable breaks. If you have a cable break in a cross-wind, turn off to the downwind side to give you more room. You will not need a complete circle to land into the wind, but check the ASI and use a well banked turn. Do not use a gentle turn – this will use up more height.

the final turn, however low, calm yourself down and concentrate on making a safe landing. Look ahead and hold off properly. Bad landings almost always damage a glider.

Judging the conditions

This all sounds simple but the catch is that the conditions are so variable. Since the launch failure may occur on any flight you must spend a few minutes considering the conditions before you take a launch. The wind strength and direction are usually important factors because it almost always pays to turn off to the downwind side of the field. This gives you much less of a turn to make to get back into wind if you elect to make a turn of 360°, and a longer run if you decide to make an S-turn and land into wind. In light winds the shape and size of the possible landing area ahead will dictate what to do and where to go. Think before you fly and if in doubt or flying at a strange site, discuss the possibilities and the special circumstances before you fly.

Conclusion

Safe and efficient winch and car launches are mainly a matter of ensuring that the climbing attitude is achieved smoothly and gradually with a safe airspeed. They are much easier to do than aerotowing, and just take a few attempts to master.

With most types of glider, the tail wheel or skid should be off the ground at the moment of taking off so that the aircraft does not leave the ground at the minimum speed. The climbing angle can then be allowed to steepen so that, if the launch fails at any moment, the glider is in position and has sufficient speed to recover into a normal glide.

Fundamentally, winch and car launch are very similar except that the acceleration on the car is usually far lower than with a winch. This makes it necessary to climb away much more gradually from a car launch.

11   Other launching emergencies

There are various possible emergencies which might occur on a launch and which are worth discussing. Even today when everyone is taught to use a comprehensive pre take-off check, far more problems arise from faulty cockpit drills and other piloting errors than by mechanical failures.

Good habits will prevent most of these accidents. In the UK cockpit checks have been standardised throughout the gliding clubs. They are rememberd by the mnemonic **CBsiftCB**. Student pilots are expected to learn these checks and to do them systematically before every take-off. Forgetting any item may cause serious problems during the take-off or flight.

However, in spite of this system pilots do still occasionally fail to do proper cockpit checks. Usually this is caused by the pilot becoming distracted at the time or by his being hurried into the cockpit. The following are some examples of the problems caused by careless cockpit checks.

Controls

There have been numerous cases of pilots failing to realise that they had not connected an aileron or elevator, and I know of one case of the pilot failing to notice that the rudder cables had become crossed during the annual inspection. Although this is mainly a matter of correct rigging and a proper daily inspection, it is sensible to check visually before every flight and to make sure you really do get the full movements. It is only too easy to allow a seat cushion or other object to slide forward or drop into the control system so that full movement is unobtainable.

A check of the movements of the control surfaces can be made while getting into the cockpit so that only a re-check that full control movement can be obtained is necessary during the pre take-off check. I have seen several gliders taking off with one aileron disconnected and fluttering: fortunately the pilots were able to keep control and land safely. There have been a number of cases where the elevator has not been coupled up. This is almost always disastrous and can lead to a really nasty accident. Modern machines now have automatic coupling of all the controls to prevent this happening, but the sensible thing is to check all the controls immediately after rigging. Hold each control surface in turn while moving the stick. Just seeing the control surface move from the cockpit is no proof that it is correctly connected. The elevator may still move up and down even though it is not connected properly.

Ballast

Several accidents have happened because the cockpit load was so much under the minimum that the glider was virtually unflyable. There have also been fatal accidents where the pilot is believed to have been underweight and in which the glider has stalled and entered a spin at low altitude.

If extra ballast has to be carried make sure that it cannot break loose in a crash or heavy landing. Just sitting on a lead cushion does not prevent it flying forward, jamming the controls or cutting through your legs in a crash or low 'g' situation. Also, remember that for first flights on a particular type or for early solos it is important to add much more ballast than the minimum. This will improve the stability and make the flying easier.

Straps

Yes, there have even been cases of pilots failing to strap themselves in. Not many years ago a pilot went through the canopy on aerotow after being hurried off in his brand new glider. Fortunately he managed to use his parachute and landed safely but the glider was a write-off.

Many pilots fail to tighten their straps sufficiently and this can result in injury during a crash or heavy landing. Only a few years ago a Lasham K8 pilot smashed his head through the canopy, flying into violent lift in the smoke from a stubble fire. You only have to fly into really severe turbulence once to realise how tight your straps have to be and that a loose object like a camera can be a real hazard. The bottom straps should always be pulled up really tightly otherwise you may bash your head on the canopy in turbulence.

Instruments

This is probably the only item which, if forgotten, would only be a nuisance. Every pilot should be able to fly safely without the need of instruments. A cracked glass or instrument case usually causes a serious error in an ASI or variometer, and in turn a zero error results in misleading indications at every speed and height.

Problems may arise because of believing the instruments when they have failed or have not been correctly set before take-off. It is well worth while checking over the instruments before take-off just to see that they are not damaged or reading abnormally. If you fail to realise that your batteries are flat and your variometers rely on power, this will certainly spoil your chances of doing well on that flight.

Flaps

On many modern machines the ailerons and flaps move up and down together when the flap lever is moved. For the best aileron control during the take-off roll the flaps and ailerons need to be at a negative angle. If you forget to set them correctly before take-off it may result in a wing-tip touching the ground and a violent ground loop. As soon as good control has been established (usually when the tail has been raised) the flaps can be lowered to help the aircraft to leave the ground.

Trim

Glider trimming devices are generally rather crude, and failure to trim with a spring trimmer may not be critical. However, a pilot unfamiliar with a particular type of aircraft could get into serious difficulties taking off with the trimmer set full nose or tail heavy. Trim tabs are usually more powerful than spring trimming devices so that a big error in setting the trim could result in the pilot having difficulty in overpowering the control loads.

Canopy

Failing to lock and check the canopy correctly can be very expensive. Moreover, if the canopy comes off it can easily crash through the tail on its way. This happened to me once and I finished the flight on a parachute, which is why I am so concerned that this item should be checked correctly.

Always lock the canopy, check the locking visually and then push up on the perspex above your head to ensure that it is really secure. In this way you are also checking the hinges and the security of the perspex itself. Over the years I must have seen literally dozens of canopies come off during take-off, none of which would have happened if the pilot had checked by pushing up on the perspex after locking. Adopt the habit now and you will never have this maddening and expensive kind of incident. I would rather make a few greasy finger-marks on the canopy than have a broken canopy. Remember that a new canopy is an expensive item and that you cannot fly the glider again until it has been replaced.

Many canopies are spoilt needlessly by people putting their hand through the clear vision window to reach the release knob while the glider is still being towed out of the launch point by car. Any sudden bump puts a load on the perspex and is likely to cause a bad crack. If this does happen the crack must be properly stopped by drilling a tiny hole just off the end of it. Otherwise the crack may spread on the next flight.

It is unwise to tow or move the glider with the canopy open as it will be broken if the securing strap breaks. Canopies should be locked down between flights so that they cannot be blown open.

Brakes

Two things can cause the airbrakes to open in flight: failing to lock them properly and a faulty locking device. Never check that the airbrakes are closed by just pushing the lever forward. If the lock is very tight the airbrakes can still be unlocked even though the handle seems forward and the brake caps are flush with the wing surface. Always open the airbrakes fully first, checking that they do both open of course, and then close and lock them. If you cannot feel them locking positively the lock is badly adjusted and there is a risk of the airbrakes flying open if you get a sudden bump. If one side is opening before the other it is possible for the suction on the unlocked blade to pull through the lever system and unlock the second side. So the airbrakes must unlock and open together and the lock must be positive.

Almost all forms of airbrake have an 'over centre' type of lock and if the airbrakes can be closed and locked without feeling the mechanism locking, the machine is definitely unserviceable until the lock is re-adjusted. Sometimes the force required to lock the airbrakes on the ground is too high and an adjustment is needed. Incidents of pilots taking off with the airbrakes unlocked so that they fly fully open and spoil the launch are most likely when flying an unfamiliar glider. If the airbrake system is unusual, make sure that you understand exactly how the locking works before you take off.

Summary

Remember these checks only take a few moments but they must be done correctly in the set order to be certain that nothing is forgotten. Avoid being rushed when getting aboard and ready for your launch. If there is a hold-up and you open the canopy to keep cool, make sure that you pay particular attention to the last two items on the check-list again before you have the cable re-attached. Otherwise you run the risk of leaving the canopy or the airbrakes unlocked.

Launch failures and cable breaks have been covered in detail in a previous chapter, but there are several other situations to do with launching which can be hazardous and which need thinking about.

Hang-ups

Although extremely rare, it sometimes happens that the cable cannot be released after the launch. This situation is particularly dangerous and should be considered carefully by every glider pilot.

The most common cause of a 'hang-up' is the glider being jerked forward at the start of the take-off run so that it over-runs the cable or rope end. Unless it is very stiff, the rope (or the parachute if it is a winch of car launch) may be caught by the main wheel and wound around it.

There are several other possible causes. On one occasion I saw a Foka glider launched on the aerotow hook by mistake. Unfortunately the pilot did not pull the release knob hard enough to drop the cable and, of course, these aerotow hooks do not normally have an automatic release. In this particular instance the pilot was unaware that he had a hang-up until the end of the cable caught an obstruction. Luckily he managed to release it, but the cable fell across some power cables, causing damage and a great deal of inconvenience to the local villages.

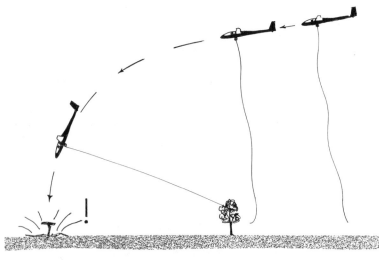

Hang-ups are dangerous!

On another occasion an inexperienced bystander hooked the glider up on the open 'bungee' hook, where it jammed solidly. As the launch was an aerotow the pilot soon discovered that he could not release, but he was able to break the rope. Of course if the launching rings are the incorrect ones or are bent they may also become jammed in the release. Never use links of chain or home-made release rings. (Incidentally, an open bungee hook can be a serious hazard if the rope or parachute gets caught on it. They should be cut off flush and the normal release used for any bungee launches.)

However, by far the most likely hazard with the modern gliders is on aerotow. If the release hook is just ahead of the main wheel any jerk in the rope can result in an over-run, with the possibility of it becoming caught in the wheel or undercarriage structure. Unless the take-off is stopped there is a real risk of the glider zooming up out of control, pulling the tug into the ground.

If you think the glider may have over-run the rope on take-off, release at once. If the release does not work try to keep the glider on the ground and to break the rope. If the tow continues, attempt to keep the glider in position. In particular, try to prevent any nose-up movement which might get out of control. Concentrate on keeping in position and do not attempt to signal to the tug pilot or do anything out of the ordinary until you have reached a height of several thousand feet.

Signalling systems

In the United Kingdom the signal to the tug pilot is to move to the left and attract his attention by rocking the wings and yawing. The tug pilot will then release his end of the rope for you to bring back to the airfield. In this case it is vital to approach with sufficient height to ensure that the end of the rope clears any obstructions. Extra speed should be used on the approach so that there is a better chance of breaking the rope or pulling it clear if it does catch on something.

The most important precaution to prevent this kind of trouble on take-off is a positive signalling system. It must be possible to stop a launch after the glider has moved forward a few yards. Stop signals such as putting the wing-tip down on the ground are useless once the machine has begun to move and, without a signaller well ahead of the tow plane, it is unlikely that the tug pilot would see the signal once he has opened the throttle. Taking off from a runway, it may be necessary to apply a little wheel brake at the start of the take-off run to prevent an over-run if a jerk does occur.

If the glider does over-run it is vital that the launch is stopped just in case the rope has become caught somewhere. Fortunately although hundreds of over-runs occur every year, it is extremely rare for a hang-up to occur and even more rare for the launch not to be stopped in time. The pilot should always pull the release and shout 'Stop' if he thinks he may have over-run. However, he cannot always see what is happening and be sure of the situation and therefore it is even more important that anyone seeing a glider over-run should shout 'Stop' and that the stop signal should be given immediately. Of course the pilot hearing a shout of 'Stop' must release at once even when he cannot see a reason for doing so. (This is because the stop signal may have been given for some totally different reason such as to avoid a hazard from a low-flying jet which had not been spotted before the launch was started.)

Aerotowing

Another type of hazard occurs when the rope end floats back and becomes caught in the undercarriage. This is usually caused by a slack rope at the time of release on aerotow. However, it is dangerous to put extra tension on the rope before releasing or to start to turn off before the rope has been seen to go since this can easily result in tipping the tow plane if the rope fails to drop off. When releasing from aerotow make sure you are clear to turn, identify the release toggle and pull it twice hard, and re-check that the rope has gone before making a climbing turn. (In the United Kingdom this turn can be in either direction.)

Winch or car launches

On a winch or car launch, if the glider over-runs and is launched by the wheel instead of the usual hook it will zoom up into an extremely steep climb in spite of the attempts of the pilot to prevent this from happening. If the glider can be kept on the ground this is definitely the safest place to be, and the winch or car driver will soon give up if the glider is held down for more than a few hundred yards. Once the nose rises, however, it may be impossible to stop it zooming up far too steeply, and the cable is quite likely to break. Fortunately with the stick already right forward there is a good chance of recovering and making a safe landing.

With a hang-up on a car or winch launch, it is vital to get and keep some slack in the cable. If the glider flies on until the cable becomes tight it will be pulled into an ever-steepening dive. On a windy day, side-slipping or S-turns into wind over the winch or car with the airbrakes open would greatly reduce this risk. Since the glider pilot cannot tell for sure whether the cable has been guillotined or released at the other end, he should circle keeping close to that end of the field and avoid flying over any obstructions which could conceivably catch the end of the cable. Once the cable starts to trail along the ground the drag will be very high and a steep descent will be necessary to maintain enough speed for a safe landing.

The situation is still more traumatic if it is caused by the release jamming in some way. Then the glider pilot is unlikely to be aware of the emergency until the cable becomes tight and starts to pull the glider into a dive. A natural reaction will be to pull back to try to stop the dive and the steady load, although increasing, may be insufficient to break the wire. Here the best solution may be to try to break the weak link with a sudden snatch. Pushing forward to steepen the dive still further will slacken the wire and build up speed so rapidly that a quick pull-out will almost certainly break the weak link or cable or pull it free. However, do not forget that it is still possible to be trailing a length of cable which could catch something on the ground and pull you down. Keep over the open field and fly fast until you are safely on the ground.

The Ottfur release

At one time hang-ups were one of the greatest hazards in gliding. Then Ottley and Furlong got together to devise the 'Ottfur' release – 'the hook that made gliding safe'! This and similar types of hook are now universally used for winching and the chances of the release failing are almost eliminated provided that the correct rings are used on the cable end. Thus if the pilot fails to operate the normal release the automatic or override system comes into operation and releases the cable.

However, now that it has become acceptable to put the hook right in front of the main wheel the risks of a tangle are quite high. So make sure your signalling system is efficient and can stop a launch if there is an over-run. Treat every over-run as a potential hang-up and stop the launch. Be sure that you and everyone else concerned understands what to do if a hang-up actually occurs.

Remember, you may never see a hang-up in the many years you fly but the danger is always there and it needs to be considered seriously.

12   Circling technique in thermals

Nothing is more frustrating than taking a launch on a perfect day when all the other gliders are up soaring and then falling to earth almost as quickly as the tow plane. Yet this is what many beginners experience day after day until they either give up altogether or take a dual flight with an expert to learn how to use the thermals.

Learning to turn

In almost every case the cause of the trouble is that the pilots are not turning steeply enough. Most people realise that the rate of sink of the glider must increase as the angle of bank gets steeper. Quite naturally they conclude that steeper turns cannot possibly be efficient for soaring. Others genuinely believe that they are turning tightly enough when in reality they are only using 10–15° of bank.

Many pilots are apprehensive about turning steeply at low speeds for fear of stalling and spinning – mainly because they have never explored stalling thoroughly during their training. You will never make a successful soaring pilot while you are inhibited about steep turns, and the first step in overcoming this problem is to go up and practise much steeper turns than you think you will ever use when soaring. Try about 60° of bank: unless you measure the angle you get you will probably be nearer to 45°, but that is a step in the right direction. The point about practising very steep turns is that they make turns of 30–40° of bank seem quite gentle and normal.

Practise slowing down until you can feel the pre-stall buffet and try flying on the edge of that buffet. Then experiment by pulling back further. If you are turning really steeply you will find it difficult to stall sufficiently to drop a wing, and the slightest relaxation of the backward pressure on the stick will effect an instantaneous recovery. Since the stalling speed is so much higher in the well banked turn, the controls remain responsive right up to the moment the wing stalls, and any movement forward unstalls the wing immediately, giving you full control again. Not so in a gently banked turn. Here the stalling speed is much lower and you have to regain speed before you recover the good handling after the stall.

Getting the feel of the glider

You need to know what your glider will do when you take it too slow in a tight turn. Most types just buffet and roll slightly but are controllable so that even with the stick right back the stall is still undeveloped. A few types will stall sufficiently to drop a wing and try to spin, but this is not normal in modern machines unless excess rudder is being used or the stick is snatched back violently during a turn. Whichever type of glider you fly you will not soar well until you can confidently fly to the limit, and you will not have much confidence unless you have explored the behaviour of the glider as it stalls in the turn not just once, but many, many times.

Speed

In most cases the best speed for well banked turns (30° or more) is just above the buffet speed for that angle of bank. In very turbulent conditions you will need a few knots extra to improve the handling and to avoid stalling in the gusts. Extra speed increases the radius of the turn preventing you from using the best cores of lift and reducing your chance of staying in a weak, small thermal. The speed must be kept down for efficient thermalling and the way to find the right speed is to get your turn going and then slow down until you feel the start of the buffet. Next, add a few knots and keep to that speed, no faster.

Practise getting into the turns very quickly. If you apply the bank slowly the glider will have flown some distance away from the lift before you get the turn established, and you may lose it altogether. It is vital that the turns are concentric or you will move out of the lift. Bank and speed must be constant. If you can turn fairly steeply and accurately this will improve your chances of being in the lift you aimed for.

Reading the variometer

Remember the effects of the variometer lag. If you wait for the maximum reading you will have gone well past the area for best lift. Don't delay; get turning as soon as you realise that you are in lift. The first turn as you fly into lift is particularly critical. If as you turn the lift changes to sink, only a minimum of height will be lost if you have used a well banked turn. The rate of turn is so high that it takes only a few seconds to make a circle and start to re-centre. Furthermore, a well banked turn is much more likely to keep you inside the lift. A gentle turn almost always takes you out into the adjoining sink and it will cost you dearly as you turn slowly round to a position from which to straighten up and re-centre.

Expensive and elaborate variometers do not have any significant advantage for working thermals. What is essential is good total energy compensation so that errors in maintaining a steady attitude and airspeed do not cause misleading indications on the variometer. Even experts do not keep the speed within a few knots in turbulent conditions. Of course an audio-variometer makes it all a little easier and allows you to concentrate more on the attitude of the glider.

Even with modern variometers thermalling is a game for quick thinking and quick reactions. However, these are not so essential if you programme some of your actions ahead of time. Thus, as you approach under a likely-looking cloud you could be looking around to make sure that you are not too close to any other gliders and decide which direction you will turn if you do not get any obvious tipping. You will be expecting some slight turbulence as you fly into the edge of the thermal and as you feel it you can glance to check the variometer readings. The instant you feel an upward acceleration and see the vario-needle moving up towards the zero mark you can be ready to apply the bank quickly. Contrast this with the time it would take you to look around, decide which way to turn, think whether you are going to bother to try a circle and then apply the bank. By then you may be several hundred yards away from the area of lift.

Centring

Many of the best thermals have the property of self-centring a glider which is turning in a well banked turn. This is because of the effect of the vortex flow which produces an inflow in the lower regions of a thermal bubble. A well banked turn allows this effect to work and your glider will often find its own way into the best lift if you keep turning steadily. However, this effect becomes almost non-existent if you turn with less than 20° of bank and often you will miss a strong, narrow core altogether if you circle so widely. Of course if you are flying at 3,000–4,000 feet the areas of lift are often very large and technique may not seem to matter, but the pilot who searches out the really strong cores wins the day and usually this will involve turning steeply.

A very useful and quick method of centring once you are in lift is just to steepen the turn swiftly as you feel any surge of stronger lift. This immediately moves the centre of your turn towards the better area. To use this method effectively you must be able to enter a very steep turn quickly and to hold it accurately at minimum speed for at least a full circle before opening out gradually to a more reasonable angle of bank. The beauty of this method is that it does not involve any orientation or allowance for variometer lag. If you are skilled enough at instrument flying you can use it to centre on lift in cloud.

Eventually the actual flying of the glider becomes almost automatic and you can devote much more attention to the really important job of looking for indications of better lift and making the best use of it.

But however experienced you may be it is vital to accept that circling below 500 feet is never without risk. No matter how well you handle the glider there is always the possibility of being fully stalled by a severe gust in the edge of a thermal. Remember the adage of the Tiger Club, a famous sport flying club in England: 'All aircraft bite fools.'

Rules for successful thermal soaring

1.   Search below the best looking cumulus within easy reach.
2.   Turn as soon as the variometer confirms that the acceleration you felt was lift. Do not wait for it to show a climb.
3.   Apply the bank quickly, use a well banked turn (40°) and circle at low speed (just above the pre-stall buffet but sufficient for adequate control).
4.   Never wait for the highest reading on the variometer – by that time you will always be past the best lift.
5.   Keep the bank and speed constant.
6.   Do not increase speed in sink while turning.
7.   Never reverse the turn except to conform with other gliders.
8.   Move away from any poor part of the circle, making a small correction on each circle.
9.   Tighten up the turn when the lift feels good or you experience surge of lift.
10.   Keep a sharp look-out especially when you are climbing well. Everyone will come and join you.

13   Safety aspects

Looking around

There can be no doubt that the risk of collision is still the greatest hazard in gliding. But it is unusual to hear of any real advice being given to student pilots on how to minimise this risk. True, most gliding instructors are insistent that their students look around before every turn, but this is often all that they do.

In spite of the exceptional all-round view from the cockpits of most gliders, it is surprisingly easy to miss seeing nearby aircraft. The following are a few hints which may help to improve your chances of spotting other aircraft and reducing the risks of collision.

It is difficult to spot other aircraft if you look around, scanning the sky in a continuous sweeping motion. This is because it is easier to see a moving object in the distance if you hold your head still for a few seconds so that any movement shows up against the stationary background. It is also a fact that the brain does not always respond to messages from the eye unless the object sighted is near the central part of the visual field. So whenever possible look around by moving your head in stages, holding it still for a few seconds and then moving round to search the next area.

Focusing

Aircraft which are on a collision course to you are the most difficult to see because they remain in a stationary position relative to you, like a mark on the cockpit canopy. If the other machine remains in a constant position, you must make it move.

A further difficulty is that the eyes do not automatically focus for distance after a glance at the instruments or a nearby object. Try to look back to a distant aircraft or even the wing-tip before looking for other gliders. Once you have spotted another machine, the problem becomes one of deciding whether it is likely to be a hazard. Aircraft which appear to be above your horizon are above you; those below the horizon are lower than you. So with gliders in non-soaring conditions it is the ones on your level or above that are most important to watch. Unless you deliberately lose height quickly anyone well below you will remain below. (Most gliders have very similar rates of sink.)

If you have ever flown radio-controlled model planes you will know that sometimes you get an ambiguous view of an aircraft and cannot, for a few seconds, tell if it is coming or going, or turning one way or the other. Watch for any change in the size of the aircraft and do something immediately if it is getting bigger. Never assume that the other pilot has seen you or that he will take evasive action. Pulling into a turn will probably give him the best chance of seeing you and get you away from him, but try not to lose sight of him as you turn.

Be careful not to concentrate all your attention on the one aircraft you can see. It is always another one that is the real menace. Once you have decided that a particular machine is well clear, re-check its position from time to time but watch out for others.

Joining other gliders

Blind spots

Every type of aircraft has some 'blind' spots and it is particularly important to recognise when the other pilot cannot see you. If you can see his face, he can certainly see you (if he looks). Never fly directly above or below another glider – it may pull up or dive at any moment. Following above or just behind another machine is particularly dangerous. If the pilot pulls up in front of you he will lose speed so rapidly that there may be no way to prevent a collision.

In the thermal

Of course gliders in the same thermal should always circle in the same direction, but it is also best for any glider using lift nearby to circle in the same direction. You will almost always end up together in the same part of the thermal and this is far easier if you were all going in the same direction in the first place.

When you are thermalling keep tabs on all the nearby machines. If you are out-climbing them unless they are idiots they are bound to come and join you.

Gliders coming into your lift at about the same level or below you will generally be well below you when they arrive. You will have been climbing whereas they will usually have lost some height as they go through the adjoining sink. The ones slightly above your level are the most likely to be a problem. They will appear to sink down to your level as they arrive. This does not matter if they are joining correctly by making their first turn wide before pulling into your tighter circle. Watch out if they look as though they are going to cut across your circle or are flying at high speed and may pull up steeply. Be prepared to take evasive action.

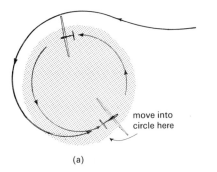

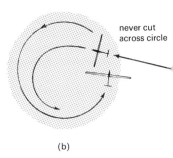

(a)

(b)

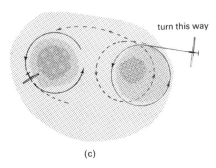

(c)

Joining other gliders in thermals (1). (a)   Always join outside their circle and only move in when on the opposite side. (b)   Never join by cutting across another pilot's thermal. (c)   Always circle in the same direction as any nearby glider to make joining each other safe and simple.

Do's and don'ts

Never cut across the circle when joining another glider or gaggle. Make sure that they have had ample opportunity to see you before you tighten up your circle. It is a pleasant gesture to wave across to any pilot joining your thermal and nice to receive a friendly wave back in acknowledgement. If I see no reply I assume that the other pilot is not looking around enough, and I keep well clear of him. Similarly, if I see another powered aircraft passing by I always wag my wings to show that I have seen him. Usually I get a reply and it is a comfort to know that they are keeping a good look-out too.

There will be occasions during thermalling when you will lose sight of a nearby glider because it is directly behind or slightly above or below you. Never continue circling, trusting that the other pilot can see you and will take evasive action. Straighten up and leave the circle without delay. Then turn and check that it is clear before rejoining. In the meantime the other pilot may have gained a few hundred feet but it will be easy to get back into the lift by using him as a marker. Never allow another glider to thermal just above or below you. The horizontal gusts in a thermal will affect each machine differently and can result in one of the gliders being lifted or dropped on to the other with no possibility of avoiding a collision. Sometimes at lower altitudes it may be possible to discover where that other glider has gone to by spotting the positions of your shadows on the ground below.

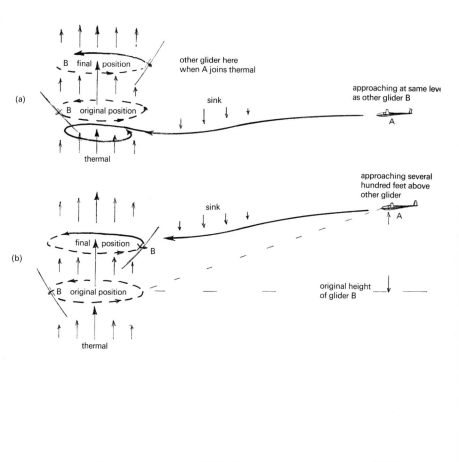

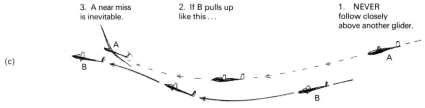

Joining other gliders in thermals (2). (a)   Gliders thermalling at your level will usually be well above you by the time you arrive. (b)   Be cautious when approaching gliders which are lower than you. (c)   Never follow closely above another glider.

Other hazards

Never climb right up to cloud base with other gliders nearby. Clouds have a nasty habit of forming all around you and several machines may be enveloped in cloud in few seconds. Remember, you cannot possibly avoid something you cannot see. Cruising along very close to cloud base is also a crazy thing to do. It only takes two of you with the same idea to produce a potentially lethal situation. Either call on 130.4 and continue climbing on instruments, or stay several hundred feet below any wisps of cloud so that you can see and be seen.

Ridge soaring is particularly hazardous unless every pilot is alert and knowledgeable. In hazy or cloudy weather modern gliders with their very small frontal areas and thin wings are particularly difficult to spot head-on. Meeting head-on at or about the same level, the glider with the hillside on his left must give way and move out sufficiently to give the other pilot plenty of room to pass. Again, never pass close above or below another glider and never creep around those blind corners hoping that no one is coming round the other way. There are, of course, other additional rules specific to hill soaring which may vary from site to site. If you fly abroad make quite sure that you know their rules for hill soaring. For example in Germany an overtaking glider flies out away from the ridge to pass another machine, not between the other glider and the hillside.

As well as just seeing and noting the positions of all the traffic nearby, you really need to be anticipating their likely movements and how much they will affect you. For example you should be able to predict whether that nearby glider is just about to turn back towards the airfield or start his circuit, and arrange to be out of his way so that neither of you has to take evasive action. This will allow you to pay more attention to other parts of the sky or to other aircraft.

Other local traffic

It is useful to note every launch and to see where each glider goes. Watch out for powered aircraft and tug and glider combinations taking off as they are less predictable than gliders. Remember in which direction they go and look for them as they come back. Descending tugs are particularly unpredictable and often the tug pilot has a very restricted view.

Try to anticipate circumstances which will intensify the traffic in your area. For example a squall line or heavy shower will usually result in a large number of gliders rushing back for a landing. There is little point in staying up a few extra minutes. Get down ahead of them and before the heavy rain arrives. It may cut the visibility down to a few hundred yards and reduce a glider like the Nimbus to the same level of perform-ance as a K8.

The circuit area, base leg and approaches to any airfield are always more congested, requiring special vigilance. Always assume that the other gliders and powered aircraft have not spotted your machine. Try to think ahead and avoid having other machines just in front or behind you by keeping some extra height in hand ready to join the circuit. This gives you the option of joining immediately or holding off for a while to allow the other gliders to get ahead of you.

When two gliders are rather close together opposite to the landing area it is usually best if the lowest pilot 'shows his hand' by turning in early, using his airbrakes to get down quickly so that the other pilot has plenty of time and room to choose his approach and a clear landing area.

There will be very few of us who will not, at some time, have the alarming experience of suddenly seeing another aircraft frighteningly close, having failed to spot it until the very last moment. Treat it as a serious warning. Talk it over with the other pilot. Did he see you? Admit that somehow you missed seeing him and try to analyse how and why it happened. Never belittle such a near miss; take the hint – consider yourself lucky to be alive. I do!

14   Variometers

Besides the usual ASI, altimeter and compass, gliders have specialised instruments for indicating the rates of climb and descent much more rapidly that the customary VSI fitted to powered aircraft. Glider pilots are particularly interested in knowing exactly what the rate of climb is in very weak lift when the glider may only be gaining a few feet per minute of height. Also, in order to know exactly where the lift is strongest the response must be very rapid. The instruments used to indicate these factors are known as variometers, and they are the most important instrument for the glider pilot.

Basic design

Most simple variometer systems consist of an insulated container known as the bottle or capacity (usually a vacuum or 'Thermos' flask) connected to the panel instrument. As height is gained the outside atmospheric pressure is reduced and becomes less than the pressure inside the flask. This starts a flow of air out of the flask along the tubing and through the instrument which indicates the rate of climb in knots (hundreds of feet per minute) or in feet or metres per second.

Early models

In the very early instruments such as the Cobb–Slater variometer, the airflow was fed into tiny plastic tubes containing a red and green ball. When gaining height the green ball was lifted up its tube and when losing height it went to the bottom and the red one was raised. By tapering the tubes the leak of air was increased as the ball was lifted.

More recent versions

More modern instruments are often of the 'vane' type. In these the air flowing to and from the capacity deflects a small vane attached to the pointer. A hairspring centralises the vane and as it swings the position of the vane regulates the amount of leak, ensuring that the calibration is both accurate and linear. It is remarkable that such minute flows of air can be measured like this with such a simple mechanical instrument.

However, for a very quick response the movement of the air can be detected electrically by thermistors or, in more recent times, by means of transducers which measure the changes in atmospheric pressure directly.

These electrical instruments make all sorts of clever tricks possible. At the flick of a switch the scale of the indicator can be changed from a full-scale reading of 10 knots (or 1,000 feet per minute) to half or double that for special conditions. It is also easy to make it drive an audio unit.

Most gliders are now fitted with audio variometers. These indicate that the glider is climbing by a pulsing note or a series of clicks which vary with the rate of climb. A different sound is used for indicating sink. This eliminates the need to watch the variometer itself except to get a better idea of the actual rate of climb. This is particularly important when flying close to other gliders in thermals. Obviously in these situations it is a great help to be able to fly and centre in the best lift without needing to look at the instruments.

Total energy compensation

Whereas the power pilot is not too worried by the exaggerated rates of climb indicated by the VSI as the aircraft is nosed up into the climb, the glider pilot needs to know that any climb or descent shown by the instrument is caused by rising or sinking air and not by his pulling or pushing the stick.

In a modern glider flying at seventy to eighty knots between thermals, pulling up to slow down and take advantage of an area of lift may result in gaining several hundred feet in a few seconds. On a normal VSI or glider variometer this would mean an indication of 1,000 feet per minute or more, even if, in fact, there was no rising air there at all. In still air the instrument would then be showing the rate of climb due solely to the changes of speed.

Since it is practically impossible to circle without the occasional variation in speed, the effects of these inaccuracies usually result in indications on the instrument far in excess of the variations in the 'lift' (the rate of climb occuring because of flying in rising air).

During the early days of low performance gliders, the effects of pulling back on the stick to make the variometer show a climb, known as 'stick' lift, were not very serious. With a modern glider, however, they would be hopelessly confusing .

In 1949 Hugh Kendall was the first person to come up with a practical solution, compensating a variometer for these effects. He recognised the need to eliminate the readings of the instrument caused by changing speeds and devised a means of doing so, which became known as total energy compensation.

Briefly the problem is that the energy of the glider in flight is a combination of potential energy due to its height and kinetic energy due to its speed. If the glider had no drag (an impossibility, of course) the two would be exactly interchangeable. From steady flight at a given speed, diving down to a lower height would result in a certain increase in speed and pulling back would result in returning to the previous height and speed with no losses.

Whereas the normal variometer is satisfactory if the speed is constant, with a total energy variometer changes in speed do not affect the reading because the gain in speed and kinetic energy is compensated for by a corresponding extra loss of height. In normal air the readings are almost unaffected by raising and lowering the nose. Therefore putting the nose down simply results in a gradual increase in the rate of sink. At any given moment the rate of sink indicated is that which the glider would have if it was flying steadily at that speed. An interesting effect with a variometer compensated for total energy is that is does not show any climb during a loop, just small variations in the rate of sink as the speed changes.

Powered aircraft and motor gliders

Any rate of climb indicator can be made to read total energy and for gliders this is essential. Fitted to a powered aircraft or motor glider, however, total energy results in a false indication of climb if the aircraft accelerates with an increase in power. For example it will show a climb during the take-off run. This is because the aircraft is gaining energy as it accelerates. Similarly, if the aircraft is slowed down by a reduction in power the total energy variometer will show a rate of descent even though no height is being lost. To avoid confusion, motor gliders often have a switch to cut off the total energy compensation for powered flight.

Total energy systems

The tube type

There are a number of methods of total energy compensation in common use. The simplest is to fit a tube type. This consists of a tube with the end blanked off, mounted out from the leading edge of the fin or above the fuselage and connected to the static side of the instrument. The tube is bent so that the airflow blows almost at right angles to it. Very close to the blanked end there are several tiny slots or holes cut into the rear side of the tube. Air flowing around the tube creates a slight suction which, of course, varies with the speed of the airflow. Thus, the tube acts as a simple venturi.

While the airspeed is constant the suction is also constant, so that changes in height are registered quite normally as the atmospheric pressure changes. However, if the nose of the glider is lowered so that the speed starts to increase, besides the normal changes of pressure due to losing more height the suction increases, compensating for the extra rate of descent caused solely by the change of speed. Fortunately the law governing the suction on a venturi provides exactly the amount of correction needed.

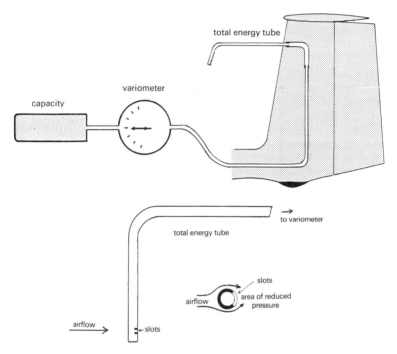

Variometers. (a)   A simple system using total energy. (b)   The total energy tube.

Transducer method

Another common system is to use transducers to feed both the pressure changes due to changes in height and the pressures in the Pitot tube caused by changes of speed into a mini computer which knows the performance of the glider throughout its speed range. This method has the advantage of eliminating the drag of the tube and the possibility of it getting iced up in cloud.

With good total energy compensation it is possible to decide whether or not it is worth circling in lift to gain height while pulling up into a steep climb to lose speed. The pull-up has no effect on the variometer readings and only the rate of climb due to the lift is registered.

The MacCready ring

Theoretical studies into cross-country speeds were made by a number of people before the Second World War, but it took the practical genius of Paul MacCready of man-powered aircraft fame to devise a simple way of presenting the necessary information to the glider pilot.

The optimum speed required to fly between thermals is very much faster than that which is needed to give the best gliding angle when good rates of climb are achieved. The time taken to fly to the next thermal and then to regain the lost height is less if flying at a higher speed, even though more height is lost in between. However, if the next thermal is a long way ahead, flying at a faster speed will result in arriving too low and perhaps having to land. Unless the pilot is almost certain that the next thermal is within easy reach and will be strong, he should compromise and choose a slower speed to conserve height and so reduce the element of risk. In competition flying the winner is the pilot who chooses the best route to avoid the worst of the sinking-air and so spend more time in rising air and who, in addition to using only the strongest lift, makes the best estimates of the thermals he is using.

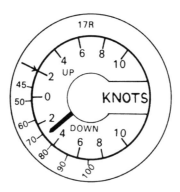

The MacCready ring. In this instance the ring is set for a 2 knot climb, with the variometer needle indicating that the speed should be 70 knots.

The MacCready ring is a movable ring around the variometer, calibrated so that when it is set for a certain rate of climb it indicates the optimum cross-country speeds. The system works for any linear scale instrument and is very simple to use. All the pilot does is to try to guess what the strength of the next thermal will be if the thermals are obviously within easy reach. The system is set by turning the ring until the index arrow is opposite the expected rate of climb. The needle of the variometer then points to the scale on the MacCready ring and tells the pilot to go faster or slower. It is not necessary to fly at exact speeds because of all the variables, but the nearer that the pilot guesses to the correct rates of climb the faster the average speed he can achieve for given conditions.

In practice the advantage gained by flying at the optimum speeds is only 5–6 k.p.h. (3–4 m.p.h.) while the lift is weak, and therefore it pays to be conservative in poor conditions. Gains of 20–30 k.p.h. (15–20 m.p.h.) in average speed are possible when the rates of climb are high.

This simple ring system is useful for giving the pilot an idea of what he should be doing on glides between thermals. In sinking air the needle points down further, indicating the need to fly faster in order to get through the sink quicker and so save height. But as the speed is built up so the normal rate of descent of the glider escalates and this indicates that a further increase in speed is necessary. Thus with this system the pilot gets involved in 'chasing the needle'.

Airmass or Netto

MacCready had the answer to this back in 1952 when he developed the Airmass or Netto variometer. He realised that if the instrument could be made to show the rates of ascent and descent of the airmass instead of what the glider was doing, the needle would point directly to the speed at which to fly instead of needing to be chased. Very few pilots thought much of the idea at first and it is only relatively recently, with the use of much higher flying speeds, that the advantages have become obvious.

Converting any variometer to indicate airmass is simple and inexpensive. A minute quantity of air is bled from the pressure side of the ASI system into the capacity side of the variometer. Usually a very fine capillary tube (rather like a hypodermic needle) is used and the calibration is done by adjusting the exact length of the tube. At a steady speed just enough air is leaked into the system to make the instrument read zero instead of the normal rate of descent of the glider (at normal slow cruising speeds, about 150 feet per minute). At higher speeds where the glider would be losing height faster, the pressure in the Pitot tube is greater, so more air flows in to compensate. In this way it is possible to get the variometer to read zero over quite a large range of speeds in still air.

The great advantage of the airmass system is that when flying at high speeds where the normal rate of sink is perhaps 500 or 600 feet per minute, it is immediately apparent if the glider flies into even weak rising air. The moment the needle rises above the zero mark the audio starts squeaking and the pilot can start to slow down. Even in quite a low performance machine, using airmass can increase the average cross-country speed and the distance covered by a significant amount.

The only disadvantage of using the airmass system is the likelihood of the pilot mistaking the indication that the air is rising for a worthwhile area of lift. An indication of even 300 feet per minute may be insufficient to make the glider climb at all if it is circling very steeply. This problem is usually overcome by incorporating a switch to turn off the air leak and make the variometer read normally during climbs. Alternatively, some pilots prefer to keep one variometer on airmass and another for thermalling.

Speed directors

It is only a short step from the airmass variometer to the director system. Instead of showing what the air is doing, the instrument is made to read zero if the speed is correct. If the glider flies into rising air the needle rises, indicating the need to slow down for optimum results. However, the pilot still has to get out his crystal ball to estimate the strength and distance of the next thermal and set an appropriate rate of climb for the instrument to work on. Like the MacCready ring, if the setting is too high the instrument will be telling the pilot to fly much too fast and time will be lost instead of gained.

Navigation computer systems

Main functions

There are now a number of very successful navigation computers coupled into the variometer systems. These combine the director and normal variometers with a computation of the height required to cover the distance to a destination or to a particular place en route. The distance through the air is measured by the variations in speed against time, and the height being lost every microsecond is also fed into the device. If an allowance is made for the wind, the instrument will tell the pilot exactly how the glide is going, whether he is above or below the glide path and by how much. This is valuable information now that gliding angles of 80:1 are possible in a following wind. With such a flat gliding angle it is quite impossible to see your destination from more than a few miles away, let alone judge whether the glider will reach it.

The computer systems can also be used to find the effective wind speed and provide a very useful aid to navigation. A switch is provided to turn off the distance-measuring during circling climbs, although the wind effects are still taken into account. Usually the distance covered will be accurate to within a few miles which is a useful aid to pinpointing the glider's position. This is rather like a DME, the distance measuring instrument used in powered aircraft which tells the pilot exactly how far it is to the radio beacon at his destination.

Other information

All the modern computers of this kind give the pilot other information as well. The average achieved rate of climb for the whole thermal and for the last thirty seconds or so are particularly useful in helping the pilot to determine when the lift begins to fade and whether it is time to rush on to the next area. Water ballast is used to increase the wing loading for faster flying in stronger conditions and this can be allowed for by the computer.

Even the deterioration in performance caused by the accumulation of squashed flies and insects along the leading edges of the wings is significant, and, at the touch of a switch, can be allowed for. This allowance is often as much as ten to fifteen per cent and was certainly the main cause of my miscalculating a final glide when I landed in a field just outside the airfield during a regional competition one year. Rain of course is an absolute disaster as far as the modern high performance machines are concerned, since they depend so much on their laminar flow wing sections.

Thus variometers have come a long way since the early days of the red and green ball. The modern glider pilot can have a lot of aids to soaring if he can afford then, but he still needs the skills involved in choosing where to look for the strongest lift and in selecting just how fast to fly between thermals. The sport of soaring is still very much dependent on good decision making and piloting skills for getting the best out of the prevailing conditions.

15 Buying a second-hand glider

No one really believes that the beautiful second-hand glider that they have just bought can be anything but a bargain. But in fact there are many pitfalls to avoid and you could be the person to take over a heap of problems unless you are aware of them. Therefore it is important to remember the lawyer's adage 'Buyer beware', otherwise you could buy an airworthy glider which is almost unusable.

Some common dodges

Consider the 'just been refinished' sales talk. An old foreman friend of mine used to say 'A coat of paint can hide a multitude of sins.' Ask yourself why it has a new coat of paint? It could be that the fabric is time-expired and you might be landed with a complete recovering job in a year or so. Fortunately it is remarkably difficult to disguise a poor repair without hours of work with filler and elbow grease. Re-finishing any machine well is expensive both in time and money and there is no such thing as a good, cheap job or a cheap Certificate of Airworthiness (C of A). Those coats of gloss finish may be all right on a motor car but they can be the start of a very real problem on a glider.

Unfortunately the fact that a glider has a valid C of A or has been completely overhauled does not mean that it is all right. Many of the older machines have put on weight over the years and this inevitably means that the c.g. has moved aft and that the range of permissible cockpit loads will have been drastically reduced. In fact some types become almost unusable when the minimum cockpit load to keep the c.g. within safe limits becomes close to or even the same as the maximum allowed by the C of A.

If you are forming a syndicate you will find that, while an average pilot may just need a little extra weight, a girl pilot may end up having to carry 27 or 32kg (60 or 70lb) to fly at all. Moreover, it will not be wise for inexperienced pilots to fly with the c.g. anywhere near the aft limit, and you may have difficulty getting enough ballast into the cockpit.

What to look for in a glider

So what should you look for when buying a glider? Obviously you must look carefully at the finish and general state of both the glider and trailer. Ask the owners to rig and unrig it for you – difficulty in rigging can be caused by distorted fittings or by a poor repair causing misalignment.

Fly the glider. Does it trim out to fly straight at both high and low speeds? Does it have persistent bad wing-drop at a stall? Do all the instruments work satisfactorily?

The glider's log book should tell you quite a lot about both its past history and its present owners. Who repaired it after any accident it may have had? Has it been well maintained with full details of repairs and inspections carrried out? Has it been flown regularly?

What about the minimum and maximum cockpit loads shown on the C of A document – are they reasonable? (Don't rely on the cockpit placards as they can be badly out of date.) A minimum of more than 77kg (170lb) is going to be a real embarrassment for lightweight pilots and may make the glider difficult to sell at a later date. Don't think that it will be just a matter of adding a few pounds of ballast in the nose. This can be quite difficult to do normally, but even more so if you want to put it in and take it out quickly for other pilots.

Pay particular attention to the results of all the previous weighings. Gliders never get lighter and any increase in the empty weight will result in the c.g. moving aft and increasing the minimum cockpit load. The weighing of gliders is notoriously inaccurate and it is not unknown for there to be serious errors in the calculations. You should expect an increase of 10–15kg (20–30lb) for any general respray job and there is something fishy about the weighing if the glider does not get heavier, and about the movement of the c.g. if that goes forward. If you doubt the figures why not write into the bill of sale 'subject to satisfactory re-weighing'. I know of at least three cases where this would have saved a lot of problems.

Cautionary tales

Recently a club bought what seemed to be a cheap two-seater. Of course it had a valid C of A so they thought it had to be a bargain. However, besides quite a number of seemingly small defects which took several weeks to rectify, the glider was grossly overweight due partly to repairs but also to the fact that it had been repainted all over. Thus the minimum cockpit load for a solo flight was well over 90kg (200lb) while the maximum was just sufficient for two lightweight pilots flying without parachutes. Of course most gliders have a semi-aerobatic category C of

A so that, when sanctioned by the BGA, some increase in the all-up weight is possible if it is reclassified and restricted to non-aerobatic flying. The club has probably spent more on getting it flyable than it would have cost to have bought a better machine in the first place.

In another instance an apparently beautiful glass machine proved to be unflyable. The more recent weighings made no sense with the c.g. well aft of the normal position. On re-weighing, the minimum cockpit load worked out to be 104kg (230lb) proving that there was a serious error in the last weighing. Quite unwittingly, pilots had been flying with the c.g. well off the aft limit in a dangerously unstable condition. Fortunately the owners took advice after finding that the glider was difficult to fly.

In this case the previous owner had sprayed the whole aircraft with a non-aircraft finish to make it look worth its inflated value. In consequence, not only was there a weight problem, but the fact that the control surfaces had been painted resulted in flutter problems. The balance of the ailerons and other control surfaces on modern machines is particularly critical and after refinishing they should be checked and rebalanced. There was no record of this having been done in this instance and it seems possible that the inspector concerned may have been unaware of the dangers involved.

Legal liability

The question arises as to who is liable for the cost of buying an unflyable machine. Is the BGA Inspector liable for failing to check the previous weighings or the work done, or for passing on an unflyable but airworthy machine? At best a court of law might rule in your favour; at worst you may be suing for money that isn't there. And worst of all in the meantime you and your partners are without a flyable machine.

So the moral is get expert advice from an independent inspector (inspectors can differ in opinion as to what is acceptable), look carefully at the log book and the C of A and don't buy a heap of trouble.

16   Which glider?

If you are considering buying a glider for the first time you need to be able to compare the advantages and disadvantages of each type. This chapter is intended to help you by describing the various older types which are available so that you can assess their features in relation to your particular needs.

Factors governing your choice

By far the greatest demand is for information on gliders suitable for less experienced solo pilots. These must be simple aircraft to fly yet should ideally have enough potential to take the pilot through to cross-country flying.

There may be a slight difference between the use of certain types (K6E, Pilatus B4) as private or syndicate gliders and their use in the club environment. Where the club fleet has several different types pilots who are relatively inexperienced may not do sufficient flying in a particular type to get used to its handling and flying characteristics. The private owner, however, will only be flying the one type and is therefore less likely to experience problems with it. In any case you should get approval from your Chief Flying Instructor (CFI) for the type you are going to buy.

Everything depends on the price and what is available at the time. Perhaps if the glider you really fancy is just out of your price range it is worth considering taking on another partner. You will find that every owner is convinced that their choice is best. The following notes may help to protect you if you meet the super salesman!

Basic features

Obviously you must have all the basic instruments; ASI, altimeter, compass and a good variometer. The modern Winter, vane type vario is almost as fast as most electric versions and much more responsive than the older PZL type. You must have a good total energy system and also, later on, a Netto system for cross-country flying. A radio will greatly increase the fun and utilisation of your glider by enabling the other syndicate members to know when the glider is going to land or whether anyone else intends to fly it that day. A usable trailer, parachute and barograph are essentials if your syndicate needs Silver C legs. Anything else is a luxury item which will have little or no effect on your enjoyment and flying.

I would consider the following types of glider suitable for any novice pilot of 30 or 40 solos operating from an airfield site: Swallow, Olympia 2B, K8, Skylark 2, Sky, Olympia 463, K6CR, Skylark 3 and 4, Pirat, K6E, Pilatus B4. (These are placed in approximate order of performance.) It cannot be too strongly emphasised that the probability of reaching the next thermal depends on the gliding angle – 30:1 is a very great improvement on 25:1.

The Slingsby Swallow

The Swallow was designed as a first solo club glider and was used by many clubs for that purpose. The wooden structure is particularly rugged and simple, making the glider suitable for very rough sites.

Design features

Aerotowing the Swallow is simple because of the quick response on the ailerons. It climbs well on the winch or car launches but the position of the nose is somewhat lower than on most gliders. The angle of the full

The Slingsby Swallow.

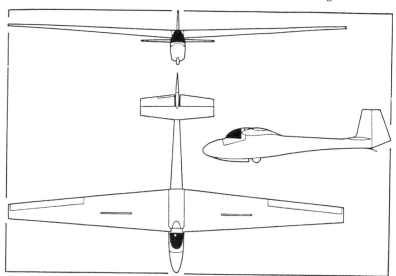

Specifications for the Slingsby Swallow.

Data   T.45 Swallow
Manufacturer   Slingsby
First flight   October 1957
Wing span   13.05m (42ft 9¾in)
Length   7.04m (23ft 1¼in)
Height   1.58m (5ft 2½in)
Wing area   13.55m² (145.9ft²)
Wing section   NACA 63₃618/4412
Aspect ratio   12.6
Empty weight   192kg (700lb)
Max weight   318 kg (700lb)
Water ballast   None
Max. wing loading   23.47kg/m² (4.8lb/ft²)
Max. speed   122.5kt (227km/h)
Stalling speed   33.5kt (62km/h)
Min. sinking speed at 36kt (67km/h)   0.91m (3ft)/sec
Max. rough air speed   75kt (139km/h)
Best glide ratio at 42.5kt (79km/h)   23

climb is best judged by looking out sideways at the wing-tip in relation to the horizon.

The airbrakes are very effective and dive limiting. They are easy to operate and do not snatch out badly at high speeds.

The cockpit is of average size in spite of the large fuselage. In particular the vertical height between the seat and the canopy is rather limited. The canopy detaches completely from the fuselage, and good habits are vital to double-check that it has been locked down securely as it is difficult to determine the exact position of the bolt after it has been locked down. A removable canopy is less convenient and more vulnerable to damage than a hinged one.

The rigging of the wings is exceptionally easy and they are very light to lift. The wings can be mounted on to the fuselage and left with the wing-tips on the ground. The wing-tips are then raised as far as they will go against a stop and a single main pin is pushed home – a super system. The tail plane is bolted down using a spanner, an adequate but somewhat old-fashioned solution.

Maintenance is excellent for a wooden glider. The structure is rugged and very simple and modern synthetic glue is used thoughout. Incidentally, many Swallows were built from kits. However, standards of home building in the United Kingdom were very high with most of the builders producing beautiful work.

Design problems

A large amount of wash-out is incorporated in the rather highly tapered wing to prevent the wing-tip stalling. As a result the performance at higher speeds is poor in spite of the alleged laminar flow wing section. The rate of roll and general handling is very good but the climbing performance is disappointing compared with the Oly 2B or K8. The best gliding angle is probably a realistic 20:1 to 23:1, but this deteriorates rapidly above about 55 knots.

The elevator range is limited and should be restricted by a stop in the gap between the tail plane and elevator to prevent a more complete stall and risk of spinning. However, even with the restriction, in some circumstances the glider will still spin for a turn or so if provoked.

Problems regularly arise when converting to the Swallow which has a relatively light elevator. Note that a very large amount of movement on the airbrake lever merely unlocks the airbrake so that the half-way position of the lever is, in effect, much less than half-airbrake. On their initial flights in a particular type of glider, inexperienced pilots frequently end up with excess speed and very little airbrake. This results in a very long float and unless the glider is held off until it has used up this speed it arrives in a nose-down attitude for the touch-down. Any bump in the ground will then cause a serious bounce whereupon the inexperienced pilot will often close the airbrakes altogether and try to put the glider on to the ground. This results in an even bigger bounce which frequently breaks the main skid and front bulkheads.

A well held-off landing using plenty of airbrake prevents all these problems which have made the Swallow unpopular in many clubs. Some Swallows have been fitted with an anti-balance tab on the elevator to increase the stick forces.

Summing up, the Swallow is a fun glider for local soaring. It is particularly suited to absolute beginners operating from small, rough and difficult sites. Most beginners should 'outgrow' the Swallow after about a year because the performance is only just adequate for Silver C flights on good soaring days.

EoN Olympia 2B and the Meise

The Olympia 2B is a British version of the German Meise and a large number of 'Olys' were built in this country by Elliotts of Newbury. The Olympia was and still is an excellent little machine, although with a best gliding angle of only 20:1 to 22:1 (measured) it is totally outclassed by later designs. The majority of the British-built ones had a fixed main wheel whereas most of the German Meise had droppable wheels leaving a long main skid for the landing. The Meise also has a smoother wing root junction giving it a better performance.

Design features

Droppable wheels are a pest as the glider becomes almost unmovable after landing and has to be lifted up to refit the wheels. Furthermore, if the wheels are dropped below about 10 feet they bounce and damage the fuselage wheras if they are dropped from above about 20 feet the wheels themselves get damaged.

The stalling and spinning characteristics are good and the nicely har-monised controls make it a real pleasure to fly.

Aerotowing is very easy with the Olympia and it is possible to send beginners off on a smooth, clear day for their first ever aerotow with just a thorough briefing, that is without any dual aerotows.

Winch and car tows are simple but the attitude is deceptive because of the angled seat-back. The full climb is best judged by the angle of the wing-tip against the horizon. During the full climb it should feel at first as though your feet are right up above your head. If the launch feels normal you will probably only get half the normal launch height which can lead to trouble on the first flight.

The EoN Olympia 2B.

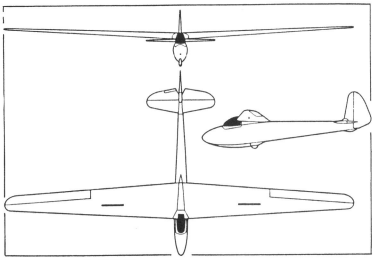

Specifications for the EoN Olympia 2B.

Data Olympia 2B
Manufacturer Elliotts of Newbury
First flight March 1947
Wing span 15.0m (49ft 2½in)
Length 6.61m (21ft 8in)
Wing area 15.0m² (161.5ft²)
Wing section Göttingen 549/676
Aspect ratio 15.0
Empty weight 195kg (430lb)
Max. weight 304kg (670lb)
Water ballast None
Max. wing loading 20.27kg/m² (4.15lb/ft²)
Max. speed 112kt (208km/h)
Stalling speed 27kt (50km/h)
Min. sinking speed at 34kt (63km/h) 0.87m (2.9ft)/sec
Best glide ratio at 42kt (78km/h) 22

The cockpit is very large and will cater for almost any pilot. The canopy is removable but has a bolt on each side which can be easily checked.

The airbrakes are very effective and dive limiting with a moderate amount of snatching if they are opened at high speeds. There is no obvious way of telling visually if the airbrakes are properly locked, and adjustment of the airbrake system is very important. Slight maladjustment with one airbrake unlocking a little earlier than the other can cause the airbrakes to unlock and open during flight. To guard against this and pilots failing to lock the airbrakes properly before take-off, the pilot should put his left hand on to the instrument panel just below the release knob during the complete launch. This ensures that if the airbrakes do open in flight the airbrake lever hits the pilot's hand, making this obvious.

The rigging is very good and both wings can be mounted on the fuselage before raising them and inserting the two tapered main pins. These must not be wrenched up with a large spanner or they will seize in the spar fittings. One finger on the spanner is all that is required while both wing-tips are being moved up and down to unload the pins.

The construction of the Oly is rather old-fashioned with large numbers of very small pieces of wood glued in place to make up the ribs and frames. All the British Olympias are glued with Aerolite which should last an infinity in that climate. A certain amount of attention is needed on the annual inspection to glue back or replace any minor sticks which have become loose. The fuselage is skinned with thin birch plywood and is a very light but strong and rigid structure. This results in a rather harsh ride on any rough ground. A fully held-off landing should be made touching down on the wheel and tail-skid together in order to avoid the risk of a violent pitch back on to the tail-skid in the event of running over a bad bump at speed with the main skid still on the ground.

Summing up, the Oly is a fun glider for local soaring. It is very suitable for inexperienced pilots and is easy to operate from small and difficult sites providing that the landing areas are not very rough. Like the Swallow it is good enough for Silver C flights, but its superior low speed circling performance makes it better in weak lift. In expert hands it is capable of 300 kilometres (190 miles) or more. It is perhaps a little prone to minor defects and damage due to poor handling on the ground.

The Schleicher K8

The K8 was the German version of the club glider. It is easy to fly and the rugged steel tube fuselage makes it suitable for the roughest sites. The low minimum flying speed gives it a similar small circling performance to the Olympia but with a better glide performance of about 24:1. This makes it ideal for early soaring flights.

Design features

The general handling characteristics are excellent. It is easy to fly on aerotow or from high winch and car launches, and the effective airbrakes make it simple to land accurately. It is forgiving and confidence building.

The cockpit is large enough to cater for most pilots wearing a parachute and for really tall ones without.

Rigging is simple and light but both wings must be held up in position until the two tapered main pins have been inserted. (A single trestle

The Schleicher K8.

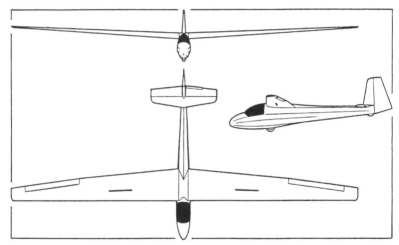

Data Ka 8B
Manufacturer Schleicher
First flight November 1957
Wing span 15.0m (49ft 2½in)
Length 7.0m (22ft 11½in)
Height 1.57m (5ft 1¾in)
Wing area 14.15m² (152.3ft²)
Wing section Göttengen 533/532
Aspect ratio 15.9
Empty weight 190kg (419lb)
Max weight 310kg (683lb)
Water ballast None
Max. wing loading 21.9kg/m² (4.48lb/ft²)
Max. speed 108kt (200km/h)
Stalling speed 29kt (54km/h)
Min. sinking speed at 32.5kt (60km/h) 0.65m (2.1ft)/sec
Max. rough air speed 70kt (130km/h)
Best glide ratio at 39.5kt (73km/h) 25

Specifications for the Schleicher K8.

under the wing makes this a relatively painless procedure.) Like the Oly the nuts on the main pins must not be overtightened.

Some K8s were assembled from kits by club members in Germany and may be slightly low-quality. However, synthetic glue is used throughout, making maintenance easy. The only problems may be surface corrosion on the steel tube fuselage.

Summing up, the K8 is the best of the older, really rugged club machines and has only been surpassed, in my opinion, by the K18 which is, in effect, a scaled-up K8 with a better wing section.

Design problems

The excellent handling and climbing performance largely offsets the poor high-speed performance which limits cross-country flights against any significant head wind. Briefing pilots for their first flight in the K8 after training in the K7 and K13, I used to say that there was only one 'catch' to the K8 – the canopy catch. Experience shows that it is adequate, but only a little safety strap prevents it being unlocked by chance with an elbow.

The Slingsby Skylark 2

The Skylark series were the first production gliders in the United Kingdom to use laminar flow aerofoils. Two Skylark 1s were made but their high wing loading made them rather too fast and difficult to circle efficiently in small radius turns. The airbrakes were abnormally powerful so that is was essential to limit the amount of airbrake being used during the round out and landing.

Design features

The Skylark 2 was produced in quite large numbers and had an increased wing area and a streamlined fuselage using glass-fibre for the nose section. This was one of the earliest production designs to use glass for a major component.

The laminar flow wing gives the Skylark 2 a much better performance than the Olympia 2B and K8, particularly at higher speeds. Even so, the best gliding angle is only about 26:1. The Skylark 2 was a very popular glider when it first came out and I can remember how the average flight time jumped as our beginners converted on to it from the Olympia 2B. It is also interesting to note that Hugh Hilditch made the first ever 300 kilometre (190 mile) triangle in the United Kingdom in one. Since then, of course, many similar flights have been made.

The Slingsby Skylark 2.

The rate of roll and the general handling is good and the large fin and rudder makes accurate turning and co-ordination easy. Like the Skylark 1 the airbrakes are still slightly overpowerful, and caution is needed when making the final approach with full airbrake. Considerably more speed is needed to complete the round out without a heavy arrival, and certainly until you are familiar with the aircraft it is wise to reduce the setting slightly. This only applies for a complete round out and landing where the final approach is steep. Full airbrake can be applied during the hold-off without trouble.

A good feature is the airbrake lock. After closing the airbrakes and pushing the lever through the over-centre lock, the handle is rotated into a recess to provide an additional lock and visual evidence that the airbrakes are correctly locked. However, even this did not stop instances where the glider takes off with the airbrakes unlocked, leading to drastic results.

The cockpit is of average size and adequate for most pilots. However, a tall pilot may find the depth of the cockpit from the seat up to the canopy rather short, and a very small pilot sitting padded well forward will also find his head is too close to the perspex for comfort. The rudder pedals are adjustable on the ground.

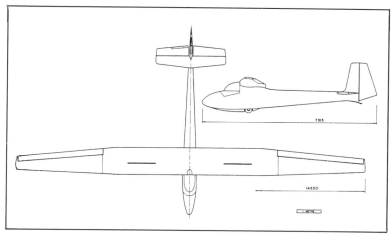

Specifications for the Slingsby Skylark 2.

Data Slingsby Skylark 2
Manufacturer Slingsby
First flight November 1953
Wing span 14.63m (48ft)
Length 7.31m (24ft 6in)
Wing area 13.37m² (144ft²)
Wing section NACA 63₃620/4415
Aspect ratio 16
Empty weight 190.5kg (420lb)
Max. weight 272.1kg (600lb)
Water ballast None
Max. wing loading 20.3kg/m² (4.16Ilb/ft²)
Max. speed 116kt (215km/h)
Best glide ratio at 48kt (89km/h) 25

Design problems

The early Skylarks had a history of losing canopies in flight because of poorly designed canopy catches. At Lasham we lost two canopies in one week, but remarkably they all just missed the tail and caused no other damage. New types of catches were designed but still they failed and it was not until the Skylark 3 came along that a really foolproof catch was produced. So check the canopy lock very carefully and always double-check it by pushing up on the perspex. A canopy can also come off if the hinges fail or if it is locked carelessly, and a new one will cost you several hundreds of pounds.

The Skylark 2 is a pleasant enough machine in the air but a pig on the ground. The small clearance between the main skid and the ground makes it impossible to lift the tail to a comfortable height and the tail is really too heavy for one person to lift. Lifting it a few inches higher the front skid is firmly on the ground, making it immovable.

The rigging is simple but the heavy centre-section is just too much for two average men to lift. Four people are needed to make it easy to lift it up over the nose and into place. In contrast, the wing-tips are very light, and with the help of a trestle or third person one man and a boy or girl can easily fit them. With the wing-tips removed the glider takes up very little space in a hangar yet is ready for action in five minutes.

The construction of the wings makes use of large amounts of gaboon plywood which resembles cigar box wood in many ways. It is much lighter than birch ply and is used in much thicker sections to provide the smoother and more stable surface needed for the laminar flow aerofoil. The structure is simple and rugged.

Summing up, only the rigging and ground handling detract from this pleasant little glider which is quite suitable for a novice solo pilot.

The Slingsby Sky

The Slingsby Sky was the last Slingsby design to use the earlier non-laminar aerofoils. Designed specifically for world championship competition, it has a good cross-country performance although it is rather slow by modern standards. The best gliding angle is about 27:1 and this, combined with the low circling speed, gives it excellent climbing performance.

The Slingsby Sky.

Design features

This is a big glider – 18 metre span as compared with the 15 metre of the Olympia and Skylark 2. As might be expected, the rate of roll is rather poor and the handling rather heavy compared with the smaller machines. The large span accentuates the adverse yaw, giving it a rather old-fashioned handling. Plenty of rudder work is needed to fly it accurately.

The cockpit is rather narrow but allows quite tall pilots to squeeze in providing that they are not too broad in the beam. Sitting in the cockpit you will immediately notice the very nose-down position, and this is a characteristic of flying the Sky which may cause you some problems on a first flight, particularly if you have a cable break and only a few seconds' flight before the landing. The wing is set at rather a large angle

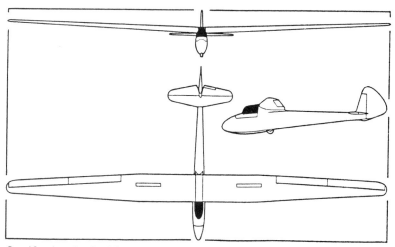

Specifications for the Slingsby Sky.

Data T.34 Sky
Manufacturer Slingsby
First flight September 1950
Wing span 18.0m (59ft ½in)
Length 7.65m (25ft 1¼in)
Wing area 17.37m² (187ft²)
Wing section Göttingen 547/NACA 2R 12
Aspect ratio 18.7
Empty weight 252kg (556lb)
Max. weight 363kg (800lb)
Water ballast None
Max. wing loading 20.9kg/m² (4.28lb/ft²)
Max. speed 98kt (182km/h)
Stalling speed 29kt (54km/h)
Min. sinking speed at 33.5kt (62km/h) 0.66m (2.17ft)/sec
Max. rough air speed 72.5kt (134km/h)
Best glide ratio at 37kt (69km/h) 27.5

to the fuselage axis so that the forward view is better than on most other gliders during a winch or car launch. This is a big glider and you will probably break the weak link or cable unless you gauge the angle of climb by the angle of the wing-tip against the horizon. In the full climb the top of the nose will still be slightly below the horizon instead of well above as in most other gliders.

The airbrakes are of an uncommon design and rather similar to those on the Blanik. They are easy to operate and reasonably effective but do not snatch like those on the K7 or K13. They have a rather soft feel and make the Sky an easy and forgiving machine on landings.

The stall is fairly docile but there will be a pronounced wing drop if the glider is skidding slightly in the turn. The spin appears to be very steep because of the nose-down attitude, but both the spinning and the recovery are quite normal. In many ways the handling and spinning characteristics are similar to the Bocian two-seater which also gives you a good view by the cut of the cockpit sides. Like the Kite 2 and Gull 4 (a 15 metre version of the Sky for all practical purposes) it is very easy to fly the Sky too slowly by putting the nose in what appears to be a normal attitude but which is really far too high.

The Sky is a tough old bird but perhaps a little more prone to damage because of its sheer size and weight. The annual C of A inspection is a big job made worse by the rather complicated cable-operated control system. The very large ailerons are divided into two with a separate drive for each portion. This is to allow the wing to flex without causing the ailerons to jam.

The rigging is heavy and trestles are recommended to avoid having to hold up the full weight of one wing-tip while the next wing is pulled out of the trailer and fitted in place. Unfortunately Slingsby's copied the Weihe's super system but got it all wrong. Unlike the Weihe the front and rear fuselage fittings are not quite in line, and lowering the wing-tip or letting one droop with both pins in place is very expensive.

Avoid the version with the dropping wheels. The tail is very heavy and even your best friends will leave you in the middle of the airfield after you have landed rather than lift that tail high enough for you to reattach the wheels.

In conclusion therefore, the Sky is a lovely old glider and a good buy for a group of pilots who enjoy doing their own maintenance and do not mind rigging and rather heavy ground handling. Phillip Wills won the World Championships in 1952 with a Sky so you can't blame the glider if you fail to stay up. However, it is a very large machine for what at best is only K6 performance!

The EoN Olympia 463

The Olympia 460 series started as a 15 metre version of the Olympia 419. The various prototypes had a small chord wing and failed to come

The EoN Olympia 463.

up to expectations because they suffered from some kind of premature breakaway of the airflow at the wing root and a sharp drop at the stall. The 463 overcame these problems and combined excellent handling and a good gliding performance – probably 28:1 or more and comparable to the K6CR in competitive flying.

Design features

The cockpit is roomy with a large removable canopy. The forward position of the main wheel makes the aircraft sit on the ground with the tail firmly down. The short skid in front of the wheel serves only as a ramp to help the main wheel over bad holes in the ground. Lifting handles are provided just ahead of the tail plane but lifting the tail is a difficult job and too heavy for comfort.

The rigging is excellent. The wings are very light with a similar wing root fitting arrangement to the Oly 2B, but with expanding parallel main pins in place of the tapered ones on the 2B. These are almost too cleverly designed and a good briefing on how to work them is highly desirable.

The construction of the 463 is unusual. The fuselage is essentially two flats with the top and bottom faired off and the nose streamlined. No one would call it beautiful but it is rugged and probably not much worse for drag than a normal rounded fuselage of the same era. The wings have a laminar flow aerofoil and a composite spar of wood and metal with the metal bonded to the wood. A special Aerodux glue is used throughout the wing to reduce warping of the plywood skins due to glue shrinkage and to avoid upsetting the wood to metal bonding which can be affected by normal acid hardeners.

The 463 has rather a short fuselage and this, together with the forward

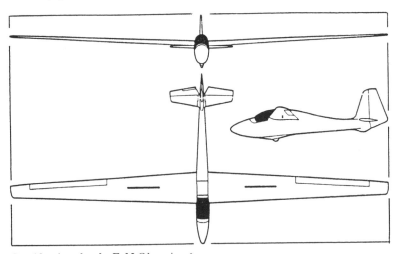

Specifications for the EoN Olympia 463.

Data 463
Manufacturer Elliots of Newbury
First flight April 1963
Wing span 15.0m (49ft 2½in)
Length 6.4m (21ft)
Wing area 12.26m² (132ft²)
Wing section NACA 64³618/421
Aspect ratio 18.0
Empty weight 181kg (400lb)
Max. weight 286kg (630lb)
Water ballast None
Max. wing loading 23.33kg/m² (4.78lb/ft²)
Max. speed 117.5kt (218km/h)
Stalling speed 30kt (56km/h)
Min. sinking speed at 37kt (69km/h) 0.67m (2.2ft)/sec
Max. rough air speed 74kt (137km/h)
Best glide ratio at 42kt (78km/h) 29

wheel position, make it far less directionally stable on the ground than training gliders such as the T21B, K13 and so on which have the wheel behind the c.g. The rudder must be used to keep straight on take-off and landing. In addition the aileron control is less powerful at low speeds and extra care is needed to keep the wings level on take-off. Usually the tail skid will not leave the ground until take-off speed has almost been reached. Therefore the stick can be held right forward to lift the tail from the start of the run whether it is an aerotow or winch or car launch.

It is wise to select a day with some wind and to avoid a calm day or a cross-wind for a first flight in this aircraft, unless of course you are experienced on similar types of glider. This will make it easier to keep the wings level and to keep straight. Caution is needed on aerotow to avoid overcontrolling. The elevator is rather light and it is quite easy to overcontrol and to set up a worrying pitching oscillation. The position of the release hook makes it very easy to get much too high on tow, but it is ideal for winch and car launching. On these the 463 climbs like a homesick angel and gives you fantastic launch height even on a short run.

The stall is reasonably gentle with plenty of warning buffet, but there will be a definite wing drop if any excess rudder is applied at the stall in a turn. A full spin will develop quickly unless the stick is relaxed forward. The spin and recovery are quite normal but it all happens rather quickly if you choose to be careless or ignore the stall warning. It should be noted that the forward view over the nose is far better than many other gliders. Beware of flying with the nose too high or dangerously slow on the first few flights.

To sum up therefore, the 463 is a nice machine to own and fly. It is easy and light to rig, climbs exceptionally well on wire launches and combines good thermalling ability with a good cross-country perform-ance. I flew one at the Nationals at Aston Down many years ago and found it able to stay with the Skylark 3s and with a well flown K6CR. A properly trained and briefed pilot of about 30 launches (solo) should have no problems. However, it needs a little more care for the first few flights and when, on a calm day, it is not difficult to drop a wing on take-off or ground loop.

The Schleicher K6CR

This is one of the outstanding gliders of all times and highly recom-mended if none of your syndicate members are tall or overweight. Unfortunately the K6CR has a small cockpit with a rather claustro-phobic cockpit canopy. However, do not despair it you are uncomfort-able in one K6; try another one (the seating does vary) and try to help matters by using one of the newer, very thin parachutes.

The Schleicher K6CR.

Design features

The handling is excellent with adequate airbrake power for beginners and for early field landings. The best gliding angle is about 28:1, fractionally better than the 463 but perhaps slightly below the Skylark 3. However, the excellent handling and climbing performance gives the K6 the advantage in most conditions. The only problem area is the directional control on the ground in light wind conditions. The forward position of the main wheel makes it a potential swinger on take-off and landing. Moving from the K8 or from a normal two-seater you must smarten up on the rudder movements and anticipate the effects of any cross-wind. The controls are all rather light but certainly not twitchy. Like the 463 you need to take care to avoid overcontrolling just after take-off on aerotow. National Champions have been known to ground loop both on take-off and landing so heed this warning and don't take chances by taking off or landing close to other aircraft or obstructions.

When the first K6 arrived we all anticipated problems because of the lack of a nose skid. Violent use of the wheel brake at very low speeds after landing can result in pitching up on the nose, but I have never seen any actual damage caused by the lack of skid apart from the paintwork getting scratched.

The only bad feature of the K6 series is the ground handling. No provision at all has been made for lifting the tail and it is quite difficult to devise a satisfactory solution. With luck your ground handling will be minimal and you can always use your car to tow it.

The lightweight two-piece wing makes rigging a pleasure, but like the K8 a trestle is needed to avoid having to hold the first wing-tip up in position until the second wing is put on and the main pins are inserted.

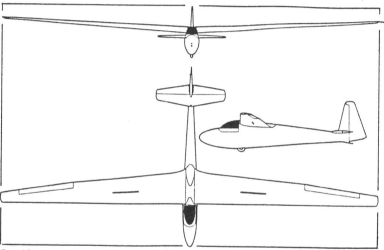

Specifications for the Schleicher K6CR.

Data Ka 6CR
Manufacturer Schleicher
First flight November 1956
Wing span 15.0m (49ft 2½in)
Length 6.66m (21ft 10¼in)
Wing area 12.4m² (135.5ft²)
Wing section NACA 63618/63615
Aspect ratio 18.1
Empty weight 190kg (419lb)
Max. weight 300kg (661lb)
Water ballast None
Max. wing loading 24.2kg/m² (4.95lb/ft²)
Max. speed 108kt (200km/h)
Stalling speed 33.5kt (62km/h)
Min. sinking speed at 36.5kt (68km/h) 0.69m (2.3ft)/sec
Max. rough air speed 76kt (140km/h)
Best glide ratio at 43kt (68km/h) 29

The main pins are plain parallel ones instead of the tapered ones found on the K8 and Oly 2B, which eliminates the possibility of overtightening them and having to use a sledge hammer to remove the pins when unrigging. (I once had to do this on an Olympia 2B!)

The construction is conventional, using pine instead of spruce. However, it is worth noting that the German manufacturers do not use cadmium plating or chromate on their metal fittings or bolts. I remember doing a ten-year inspection on a K6 and finding some of the bolts eaten away by the acid in the wood to an alarming extent, the only suspicious sign being a slight rust stain in the paint work. The British requirement of cadmium and chromate seems to provide perfect protection. The structure is slightly less complex than the old Olympia which means less regluing of the minor sticks as the glider gets older.

Thus the K6CR is an excellent choice as a first aircraft for a novice solo pilot who wants to progress quickly to cross-country flying. The only real snag is the size of the cockpit. Rigging is good, the ground handling not so good – but then you can't have everything! But the K6CR is not a K6E either in handling or performance. It is a real beginner's glider with a lot of potential and anyone can fly it.

The Slingsby Skylark 3 and 4

If you are out for performance there is still no substitute for span and most of our smaller gliders can be greatly improved by the addition of a few extra feet. For this reason it was quite an obvious development to

The Slingsby Skylark 3.

stretch the Skylark 2 to 18 metres. This inevitably results in a reduced rate of roll and very often in poor stability unless the fuselage and tail feathers are suitably enlarged.

Design features of the Skylark 3

The Skylark 3 was really a scaled-up version of the mark 2 with some improvements thrown in. The cockpit is larger and much more comfortable for a tall or well-built pilot.

This glider is very stable with rather high stick forces so that it is quite hard work to fly unless the elevator trim is used for each significant change of speed or angle of bank. The ailerons are also heavy, with the rate of roll noticeably worse than the early 15 metre machines and far worse than any of the modern designs. This takes a little getting used to and means that the low final turns can be dangerous rather than just

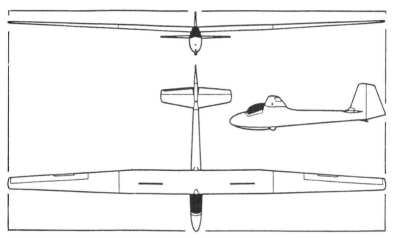

Specifications for the Slingsby Skylark 3.

Data   T.43 Skylark 3
Manufacturer   Slingsby
First flight   July 1955
Wing span   18.19m (59ft 8¼in)
Length   7.62m (25ft)
Wing area   16.1m² (173.3ft²)
Wing section   NACA 63₃620/4415
Aspect ratio   20.5
Empty weight   248kg (547lb)
Max. weight   358kg (789lb)
Water ballast   None
Max. wing loading   22.2kg/m² (4.54lb/ft²)
Max. speed   116.5kt (216km/h)
Stalling speed   31kt (58km/h)
Min. sinking speed at 35kt (65km/h)   0.56m (1.84ft)/sec
Best glide ratio at 40kt (74km/h)   30

The Slingsby Skylark 4.

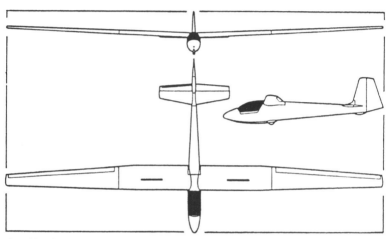

Specifications for the Slingsby Skylark 4.

Data   T.50 Skylark 4
Manufacturer   Slingsby
First flight   February 1961
Wing span   18.16m (59ft 7in)
Length   7.64m (25ft 1in)
Wing area   16.07m² (173ft²)
Wing section   NACA 63₃630/6415
Aspect ratio   20.5
Empty weight   253kg (558lb)
Max. weight   376kg (829lb)
Water ballast   None
Max. wing loading   23.4kg/m² (4.79lb/ft²)
Max. speed   118kt (219km/h)
Stalling speed   32kt (60km/h)
Min. sinking speed at 37kt (69km/h)   0.53m (1.74ft)/sec
Max. rough air speed   71kt (132km/h)
Best glide ratio at 41kt (76km/h)   32

exciting. Certainly you should give yourself plenty of height for the first few flights while you get familiar with the aircraft.

The Skylark 3 has excellent airbrakes, making it easy to land accurately. Unlike most modern machines there is very little snatch or tendency for them to suck open. As with most of the early designs the airbrakes are speed limiting in a vertical dive – if you like that kind of descent or get into trouble in cloud.

The low stalling and thermalling speeds make it a good scraper in very weak lift and the overall performance is perhaps fractionally better than the K6CR.

Altogether the Skylark 3 is a very simple machine to fly and one which is suitable for any well trained beginner. However, it is a big machine and rather heavy for both ground handling and rigging. The ground handling is better than the Skylark 2 but lifting the centre-section is a back-breaker and spoils the otherwise simple rigging.

Minor changes and the Skylark 4

There were several versions of the Skylark 3. The 'B' and subsequent models featured a longer nose, fixed main wheel in place of the optional droppable dolly wheels and various other minor structural changes. On later models geared tabs were fitted to the ailerons to reduce the heavy stick forces and finally the aileron chord was reduced which had the same result.

The Skylark 4 was the next step and involved moving the wing lower so that the fuselage and cockpit were much slimmer. The blown bubble canopy was replaced by a well contoured moulded one and the tail plane position was moved to reduce the induced drag at speeds. These changes gave the aircraft a new look and a small improvement in performance over the Skylark 3.

A Skylark 3 or 4 is almost ideal for the inexperienced but ambitious pilot. The lower wing loading makes both models easy to fly, docile and good climbers. The large cockpit makes them particularly suited to large and heavy pilots. The only drawback is the sheer size and weight of the components for rigging and ground handling. The poor rate of roll is another disadvantage but one which is easy to live with.

PZL Pirat

The Polish Pirat is in my opinion a greatly underrated machine. With a best gliding angle of about 32:1 it is superior to the Skylarks 2 and 3 and K6CR and only a little below the K6E and Pilatus B4.

The PZL Pirat.

Design features

Inspired, it seems, by the Skylark 2, the only dubious feature still incorporated in this design is the three-piece wing with the inevitable heavy centre-section. However, if a hangar is available the tips can be removed to reduce the space required.

The cockpit is very large, the ground clearance is ample and the double-decker airbrakes powerful without being unforgiving.

I had a share in a Pirat for three years and flew Nationals, Regionals and aerobatic displays in it. A few minor and inexpensive modifications were needed to make it safe for the average pilot. (They were all BGA approved.)

Without the addition of a bungy between the airbrake-operating handle and the nose the airbrake snatch loads are so high that I doubt if a young woman pilot could close them above 50 knots. With the bungy the loads are reduced and the airbrakes are easily adjusted at any speed.

I also found that the small round knobs on both the airbrake lever and the release are rather too small to grab quickly, and it was an easy matter to make larger ones out of nylon rod. The rudder pedals have rather an unusual movement which some people do not care for, but otherwise the cockpit and controls get full marks. With a 1.5m (5ft) tall woman and a 2m 90kg (6ft 8in 200lb) man in our syndicate it says a lot that both were comfortable and happy on long flights.

The Pirat handles well in every respect and meets all the requirements for an early solo and first cross-country machine. Two members of my syndicate completed their Silver C and made 300 kilometre (186 mile) triangular Diamond flights.

We fitted a total energy tube on the fin and a John Willey dolphin device to give airmass. Together these are worth at least an extra five points to the glide angle, and they enabled us to dolphin our way cross-country over long distances.

From the flying point of view I have only one real criticism. The winch/car-tow release is rather too far back. This gives superb launches but an uncontrollable initial climb when flown by a lightweight pilot. After leaving the ground it may take almost full forward stick to prevent a near vertical climb away. Do not trim forward for the take-off on a wire launch. The tab reduces the effective down movement and is better left in the neutral position as the stick forces are still quite light. The nose hook makes aerotowing simple.

The Pirat is designed and stressed for +6.3 to -3.15g with a safety factor of 1.5 and is therefore considerably stronger than most other

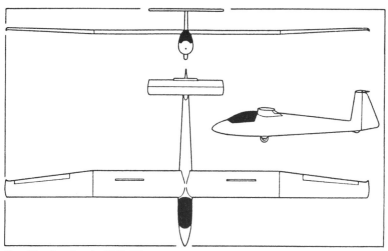

Specifications for the PZL Pirat.

Data   Pirat C
Manufacturer   SZD
First flight   January 1978
Wing span   15.0m (49ft 2½in)
Length   6.92m (22ft 8in)
Height   0.96m (3ft 1¾in)
Wing area   13.8m² (148.6ft²)
Wing section   Wortmann FX-61-168/60-1261
Aspect ratio   16.3
Empty weight   255kg (562lb)
Max. weight   370kg (816lb)
Water ballast   None
Max. wing loading   26.8kg/m² (5.49lb/ft²)
Max. speed   135kt (250km/h)
Stalling speed   32.5kt (60km/h)
Min. sinking speed at 40kt (74km/h)   0.7m (2.3ft)/sec
Max. rough air speed   77kt (145km/h)
Best glide ratio at 45kt (84km/h)   32

machines (the normal requirements are + 5.3g to -2.65g). However, in many respects the wooden structure and light steel fittings are rather old-fashioned and a thorough DI is the order of the day, particularly as these machines get older. Avoid screwing the rigging pins into the fittings as the rather soft metal can 'pick up' and score easily. Push them straight in after carefully cleaning and greasing them each time.

The only real snag with the Pirat is the heavy centre-section for rigging. Otherwise it is an ideal first machine and one of the few with a large enough cockpit.

Pilatus B4

The Swiss Pilatus is the only all-metal machine in the early solo class. One advantage of metal construction is that it can be left out in almost all weathers without serious harm. It is also an advantage in countries where the repair of wooden or glass gliders is difficult. Any metal worker can tackle minor damage and all the parts are precisely made so that replacement parts are easy to fit.

The Pilatus B4.

Design features

The B4 is beautifully built and a nice machine to fly in every respect. It has a retractable main wheel and a 'pump up' tail wheel which makes it easy to move the glider in straight lines without the need to lift the rather heavy tail end.

The cockpit is roomy and everything is much as you might expect from a country which specialises in watch and clock making.

Perhaps this is a machine best suited to a syndicate or private owner than to a club operation. The metal skins are thin and quite easily bruised or dented by careless handling in the hangar or trailer. The dents are likely to be permanent as they are difficult to remove. A little

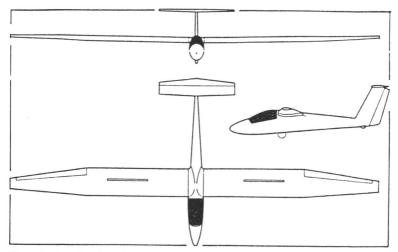

Specifications for the Pilatus B4.

Data B4-PC11
Manufacturer Pilatus
First flight 1972
Wing span 15.0m (49ft 2½in)
Length 6.57m (21ft 6¾in)
Height 1.57m (5ft 1¾in)
Wing area 14.04m² (151.1ft²)
Wing section NACA 64₃618
Aspect ratio 16.0
Empty weight 230kg (507lb)
Max. weight 350kg (772lb)
Water ballast None
Max. wing loading 24.93kg/m² (5.1lb/ft²)
Max. speed 129.5kt (240km/h)
Stalling speed 33.5kt (62km/h)
Min. sinking speed at 39kt (72km/h) 0.64m (2.1ft)/sec
Max. rough air speed 129.5kt (240km/h)
Best glide ratio at 46kt (85km/h) 35

extra care is needed assembling the glider as it is possible to bend the fairings at the wing root.

If you have never flown a metal glider you may be alarmed by the clanking noises which occur in flight. These are often amplified by the structure so that a flapping undercarriage door, for example, can sound like a major structural failure. However, there is no cause for alarm.

The B4 is a +6.3g to -3.15g aircraft and the later model has additional strengthening to allow more advanced aerobatics. The performance is very similar to a K6E, that is about 33:1 to 34:1, and the crisp handling helps to make it a good climber. The stall is well defined and the B4 will spin fairly readily if provoked. Be warned, the noise of buckling metal is alarming. However, the recovery is very positive.

To sum up therefore, the Pilatus B4 is an excellent machine in all respects and quite suitable for a well trained pilot of about Bronze C standard.

The Schleicher K6E

Although the K6E looks rather similar to the earlier K6 it has many improvements. A general cleaning up of the fuselage, nose and wing root and a far better aerofoil together with an all-moving stabiliser give it a super performance. If you can sit comfortably in the rather small cockpit this is the ideal glider to own for your first few years of soaring.

Design features

Converting to the K6E needs a little caution because of the all-moving stabiliser. The only feel through the stick is the spring force from the trimming device and this is the same at 100 knots as it is at the stall. The spring trimmer gives it only a very small force and extreme caution is needed at high speeds as it is relatively easy to overcontrol and overstress the aircraft.

The elevator is very light and it is best to avoid any sudden movement of the stick during the first few aerotows. On one of the early flights in smooth conditions it is a good idea to try out the elevator gently while gradually increasing the speed to about 100 knots. It will feel very light and rather twitchy at speed. The K6E is not really suitable for aerobatics because of the risk of overstressing it at high speeds. In other aircraft the stick forces increase with speed, making it more difficult to exceed the limitations accidentally.

In all other aspects the K6E is just another K6, so refer to the comments in the previous section (pages 115–8). All that remains to be said is that the K6E has everything to offer if you are not too large for it. Its performance makes it competitive in any Regionals and yet it is also a beginner's machine. I still envy the K6E owners.

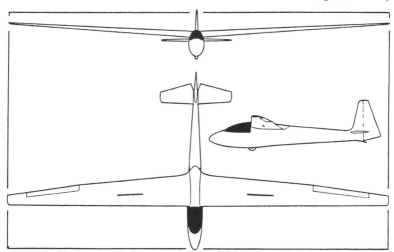

Specifications for the Schleicher K6E.

Data Ka 6E
Manufacturer Schleicher
First flight Spring 1965
Wing span 15m (49ft 2½in)
Length 6.66m (21ft 10¼in)
Height 1.6m (5ft 3in)
Wing area 12.4m² (135.5ft²)
Wing section NACA 63618/63615/Joukowsky 12%
Aspect ratio 18.1
Empty weight 190kg (419lb)
Max. weight 300kg (661lb)
Water ballast None
Max. wing loading 24.2kg/m² (4.95lb/ft²)
Max. speed 108kt (200km/h)
Stalling speed 32kt (59km/h)
Min. sinking speed at 38kt (70km/h) 0.65m (2.1ft)/sec
Max. rough air speed 54kt (100km/h)
Best glide ratio at 43kt (80km/h) 34

The ASK18

The ASK18 (or K18 as it is often known) was the last in the line of wood wing and steel tube fuselage 'club' gliders, and by popular acclaim the best ever. Unfortunately it came at a time when glass fibre machines were put into large-scale production. This meant that potential custo-mers were given a choice of the K18 or a shiny, modern-looking glass single-seater at almost the same price. Only a small number were made before production was stopped so that it is relatively rare to hear of a K18 for sale.

The ASK 18.

Design features

In many ways the ASK18 can be thought of as a stretched K8, but in reality it is a completely new design. The cockpit is much larger than the K6 or K8, making it suitable for a pilot of almost any size.

The 16 metre span and the K6E aerofoil make the performance very similar to or even better than the K6E, but without the ultra-light stick forces associated with the all-moving stabiliser. The low wing loading gives it a superb climbing ability and the performance is good enough to put 500 kilometre (310 mile) flights well within the reach of an average cross-country pilot on a good day.

Experience shows that the K18 is quite suitable as a first single-seater for beginners who have trained on a K13 or similar two-seater. It is a very popular club glider.

The forward position of the main wheel provides pilots with experience of having to control swinging and to keep straight on take-off and landing – so essential for many modern glass machines. Unfortunately, like the K6 series this wheel position makes lifting the tail to turn the glider on the ground a real pain. The tail load is very heavy, making a ground trolley highly desirable. However, it is such a popular aircraft that in spite of the heavy tail it does not get left waiting for a retrieve after landing.

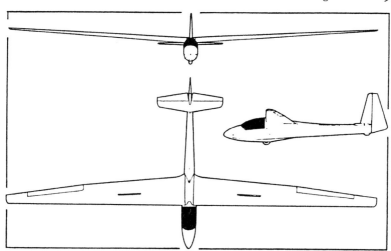

Specifications for the ASK 18.

Data ASK 18
Manufacturer Schleicher
First flight October 1974
Wing span 16m (52ft 5¾in)
Length 7.0m (22ft 11½in)
Height 1.68m (5ft 6in)
Wing area 12.99m² (139.8ft²)
Wing section NACA 63618/Joukowsky 12%
Aspect ratio 19.7
Empty weight 215kg (474lb)
Max. weight 335kg (739lb)
Water ballast None
Max. wing loading 23kg/m² (4.71lb/ft²)
Max. speed 108kt (200km/h)
Stalling speed 32.5kt (60km/h)
Min. sinking speed at 35kt (65km/h) 0.6m (2ft)/sec.
Max. rough air speed 108kt (200km/h)
Best glide ratio at 40.5kt (75km/h) 34

Many K18s were not fitted with a nose hook for aerotowing. The c.g.
hook gives superb launches on a winch or car but is rather too far back
for safe aerotowing and it is now considered essential to fit a nose hook –
a simple modification.

However, the real problem is to find a K18 available at a reasonable price.

17 Motor soarers and self-sustaining sail planes

Since a glider is a motorless aircraft it may seem strange to many readers that we have aircraft known as motor gliders. However, this kind of aircraft was called a motor glider during the early years and somehow the name has stuck. Another alternative and much more legitimate name for them is motor soarer. These are aircraft designed for soaring which have an engine to get them off the ground or to keep them up once they have been launched. Those which are not capable of taking themselves off the ground are usually referred to as self-sustaining sail planes.

Self-launchers

There is nothing new about the idea of putting an engine into a glider to make it independent of launching equipment. However, it is only since the 1960s that really satisfactory machines have been produced in numbers.

The initial idea was to produce a glider which would soar well but would also be capable of launching itself and flying cross-country to better conditions when necessary. This required a reasonable power performance but also an ability to soar well.

The early attempts were rather a poor compromise. Most of them turned out to be under-powered aeroplanes with a poor rate of climb and not a very good gliding performance. However, they were capable of flying on very low power because of the efficient, long span, glider type wing.

In the same way that yachtsmen have adopted the idea of an auxiliary engine for sailing into port it seems likely that most new sail planes in the future will have the option of a 'tuck away' engine.

There are already a number of single and two-seater high perform-ance machines fitted with engines, and they perform well.

Advantages

There are obvious advantages for the self-launcher. On the gliding site they are totally independent of any form of launching, which means that the pilot can launch when he likes and also to what height he likes. On a busy gliding site this is a great advantage for any ambitious cross-country pilot who is liable to experience a great deal of frustration at the launch point, particularly if the winch breaks down or there is a long queue of gliders waiting to go.

A self-launching motor glider also enables the pilot to climb much higher than normal to explore signs of wave or to cruise out in what would otherwise be unsoarable conditions to a hill or wave site some distance away. Pilots are finding that without the constant worry of the time wasted and the frustration caused by a field landing miles from home, they make bolder declarations and go cross-country in conditions which seem marginal but which often turn into a worthwhile soaring day. Once the engine is folded away the fun of soaring is just the same as with a normal glider.

With a two-seater, dual cross-country soaring becomes more practical because there is no need for the out landing which would normally conclude the day's flying. So the utilisation can be much higher and it is possible to go much further afield, knowing that it will only be a relatively quick cruise home if the conditions do become unsoarable. This is particularly worth while in England where the weather is so changeable.

Although these machines are more expensive than a glider or, for that matter, a normal light aircraft, they can be more used more frequently. Therefore it becomes practical to form a much larger syndicate than normal with the members still able to get more flying than with a glider. Motor soarers are particularly suited to people who have very little spare time and who don't really want to get involved with normal gliding operations. Some may live near to an airport but have to drive a long way

Self-launching motor gliders *(approximate performance figures)*				
Type	Single/ Two-seat	Span	Best glide	Speed (knots)
Scheibe SF25E Super Falke	Two	18m	26:1	46
Grob G109	Two	16.6m	28:1	60
Super Dimona	Two	17m	28:1	57
Valentine Taifun	Two	17m	28:1	60
DG400	Single	15/17m	45:1	60
ASH25E	Two	25m	55:1	60
Stemme S10	Two	25m	50:1	60

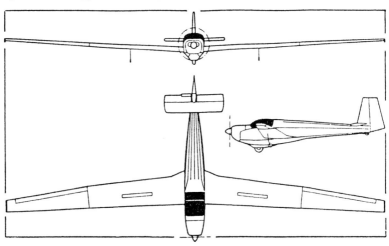

The Scheibe SF25E Super Falke.

to the nearest gliding site. What could be easier than to rig, taxi out to the runway and take off rather than waste half the day driving. With a radio, almost any airport or airstrip could be used without causing any special problems.

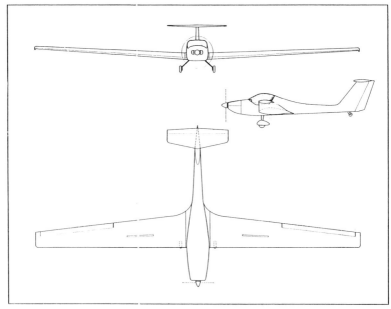

The Grob G109.

The Super Dimona motor glider.

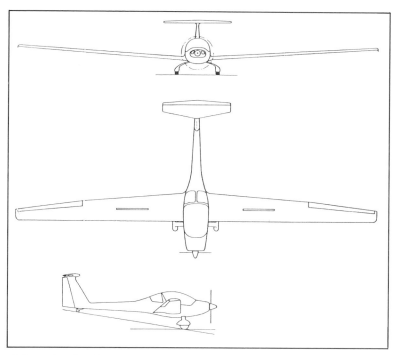

A three-view drawing of the Super Dimona.

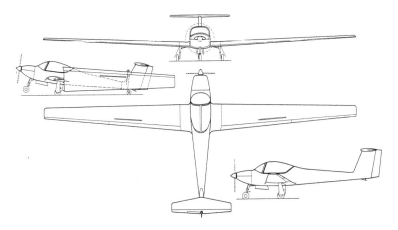

A three-view drawing of the Valentine Taifun 17E.

Problems to consider

At present many club pilots worry that these aircraft will just be used as powered aircraft for flying noisily round the gliding site or from place to place under power. However, with the present breed of self-launchers there is very little chance of this happening. In the cockpit the noise level is extremely high with the fuselage shell acting as a sound box. Ear defenders are absolutely essential and it is a blessed relief to shut off the engine after climbing to height. Also, with most of the two-stroke engines there is a certain amount of rough running when they are throttled back. This makes cruising from place to place a matter of climbing normally to height and then gliding the next 40–50 kilometres (25–30 miles) before repeating the process.

Recent developments

The first motor soarers had a simple two-bladed propeller which had to be carefully positioned in a vertical position to allow the engine and propeller to be retracted. There are now various alternatives to this system. Folding the blades allows a multi-bladed, smaller diameter propeller which reduces the propeller noise by decreasing the tip speed of the blades. The Stemme S10 is particularly clever. The nose cone of the fuselage moves forward to allow the propeller to unfold for use. The engine is mounted inside close to the c.g. and drives the propeller by a long shaft between the two pilots. Moreover, if it seems likely that the engine will be needed, it can be started and warmed up before unfolding the propeller.

The DG400 self-launching sail plane.

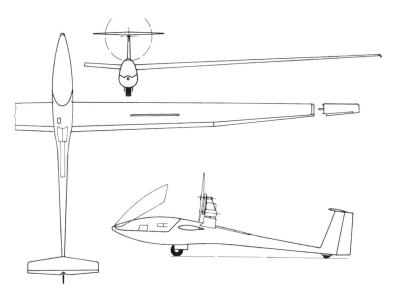

A three-view drawing of the DG400 model.

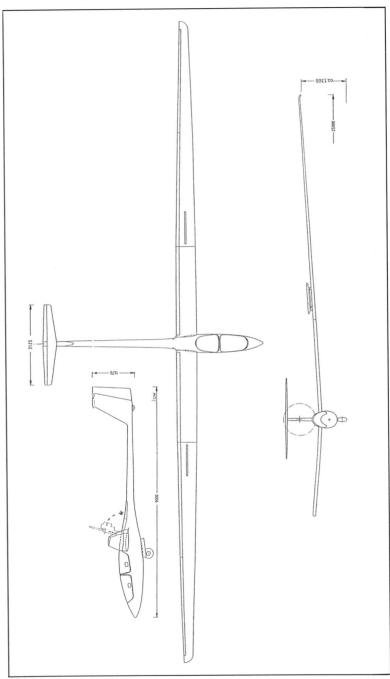

A three-view drawing of the ASH 35E.

Self-sustaining sail planes

The self-sustaining sail planes are in effect a rather less powerful and simplified version of the self-launchers. Fitting little engines to many of the best performing gliders allows them to fly home even if they are away from base when the soaring conditions fade. In producing the Turbo Discus, Turbo Ventus, Turbo Nimbus 3 and Turbo Janus two-seaters, the German manufacturer Schemp Hirth has led the field with this interesting development.

Design features

The little two-stroke engines drive five-bladed folding propellers which tuck back into the fuselage just behind the wing root, leaving no trace once the doors are closed.

One switch raises the engine electrically, the ignition is switched on and the valve lifter is operated during a gentle dive to about 70 knots. The slip-stream revolves the propeller and starts the engine. There is no throttle and the power is sufficient to give a climb of about 200–300 feet per minute or a cruise of about 70 knots.

These machines are amazingly quiet and because they do not have the power to make a normal take-off they do not require a pilot's licence like a self-launching machine. They can be launched by car, winch or aero-tow in the same way as a normal glider. Because they require rigging, ground handling and launching, the pilots have to be sociable and take a launch like any other glider pilot. In this way they are more likely to remain useful club members rather than just use the gliding club as a base for take-offs and landings.

The question has been asked whether having such a low rate of climb is safe because of the risks of running into strong downdrafts and wind gradients. However, since they are all flown by glider pilots who understand the likelihood of meeting bad sink and who are used to dealing with such situations in a glider, perhaps the risks involved are not too serious. Of course it is sensible to have chosen a suitable field and to do the restart at a fair height and not a few hundred feet up over bad country where a failure would be disastrous. At worst they can make a normal field landing like any other glider.

Machines like these offer immense possibilities for an enterprising pilot. Providing that it is landed at another gliding site, it would be perfectly practical to fly such a machine across the channel and soar down into Spain or the French Alps on one day, and on the next day to get a launch and fly home.

On an open airfield possibly all that would be needed is a tow with a car to a few hundred feet for a start and then a climb away slowly using thermals or other lift to gain height for the return flight.

With all these types, whether they are self-launching or self-sustaining, it is vital to select a field at about a thousand feet and to start a normal circuit procedure. If the engine does fail to start it is important to abandon trying to start it in plenty of time to be able to make a normal

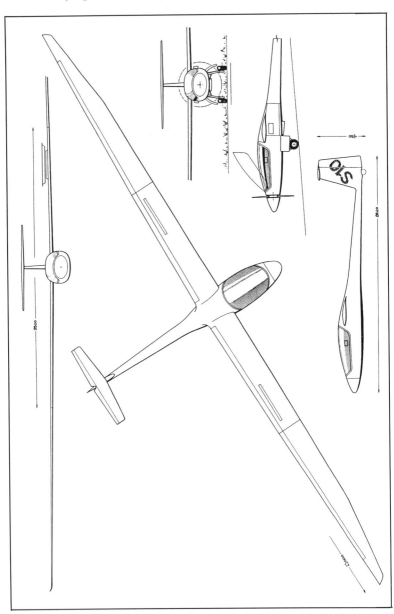

A three-view drawing of the Stemme S10.

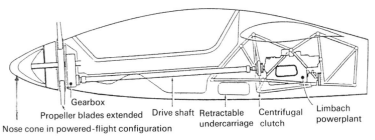

Nose cone in powered-flight configuration

Propeller blades extended Gearbox Drive shaft Retractable undercarriage Centrifugal clutch Limbach powerplant

The mechanics of the Stemme S10.

field landing. Note that in most cases the landing would have to be made with the engine up because of the time taken to re-align the propeller before retracting it. So it is essential to practise engine-up landings to get used to the much steeper gliding angle caused by the extra drag.

It must not be forgotten that with any form of electric starting and electric drive raising or lowering the engine, the system is entirely dependent on the state of the battery. Moreover, all batteries give a greatly reduced output when they are very cold. To ensure against battery failure, all these machines could do with a totally independent emergency power supply.

Doubtless there will be many improvements over the next few years which will make these machines less expensive, more dependable and easier to operate.

18   High-performance light aircraft and motor glider trainers

The present breed of two-seater aircraft with the engine in the nose is considered by many people to be more of a light aircraft than a motor glider in spite of the gliding performance being even better than many of the older two-seater training gliders.

Falkes

The Scheibe SF25 Falke series of designs showed the way to a practical motor glider and many hundreds are still flying today. These have wood wings, a steel tube fuselage and are mainly fabric covered with side-by-side seating. The modified Volkswagen car engine is mounted in the nose like a normal light aircraft.

The undercarriage can either be a single wheel with outrigger wheels to keep the wings level during taxiing, the normal two wheels with a very positive steering rail wheel or a nose wheel and two main wheels.

The Falkes have proved the value of a motor glider for all phases of glider pilot training but in addition have been used in many countries for cheap pleasure flying.

Later versions use an 80 hp VW engine. This gives the standard Falke a rate of climb of almost 600 feet per minute and a gliding angle of about 20:1. Although the gliding angle is relatively poor, the low gliding speed gives the aircraft a surprisingly good soaring performance because the small turning radius enables it to use small thermals. The tandem seating and the larger wing span Super Falke versions have a considerably improved glider performance.

Glass fibre designs

More recently, several glass fibre designs have become popular. All are basically along similar lines to the Falkes, but using modern aerofoils and taking advantage of new materials. They have conventional aircraft-type undercarriages and foldable wings to reduce the hangarage costs. This makes them very attractive and efficient machines with gliding angles of about 26:1, capable of cruising under power at over 100 knots using only three gallons per hour. Moreover, they are capable of using thermals, hill lift or wave conditions just like other gliders. However, they are not ideal for thermal soaring because their rather high minimum circling speeds and rates of sink cause difficulties in weak conditions and small thermals.

All of these types are magnificent for exploring wave systems. With the fast cruising speeds a day trip to the mountains for wave or mountain soaring is practical. Often wave is elusive and the ability to start up and fly over to the next range of hills, or to climb an extra 1,000 feet or so, makes a wave climb possible. A typical day's flying in a Falke motor glider in Scotland gave five students climbs of over 10,000 feet for only a few minutes of engine run each. The possibilities are almost unlimited.

Training with motor gliders

Why is learning to glide such a long-winded and time-consuming business?

The answer in most cases is because of the time spent between flights manhandling the glider and waiting for the next launch. Often the problems are compounded by the restricted landing grounds or by the number of gliders on the site.

Launching is usually limited by congestion so that an extra winch, car or tow plane does not improve much on the launch rate. Moreover, as the potential launch rate increases, so does the number of glider landings and these hold up the launches and block the landing areas. Each site seems to have a certain capacity for launches and even strenuous efforts do little to improve things.

The benefits

However, using the motor glider for the basic training can offer a vast increase in training facilities without increasing the congestion significantly. 'Touch and go' landings can be made, leaving room for gliders landing after only a few seconds on the landing area. Also, the motor glider can always taxi off the landing area without delay and it does not need any ground crew like a glider.

But perhaps the main advantage of the motor glider for basic training is that it releases a large number of launches for gliders. Usually a large proportion of glider launches are taken up for air experience flights and for beginners who start learning to glide and then give up for one reason or another. This severely limits the number available for other training and for solo flying.

In most British gliding clubs each member will have either an aerotow launch or two or three winch or car tows as their turn of flying. All day long members will be helping with the launching and retrieving of the gliders while waiting for their turn to fly. Often, of course, the weather intervenes and they go home disappointed.

The truth is that the majority of the people flown on any one day will never reach solo, let alone become soaring pilots. Without them the flying list would be surprisingly short and there would be plenty of launches for both dual and solo flying.

When a motor glider is used for the basic training, all of these people get their trial flights and early training in the motor glider. The people who give up during this stage have not used up valuable launches or involved the other members in pushing back the glider and organising the next launch. The result is to release a large number of launches for more solo flying and for those students who have persisted during the early stages.

During the initial handling stage, the flights will be similar to an aerotow with a climb to height followed by a glide down practising turns and so on. However, if the cloud base is too low, the instructor can still give good value by making several shorter climbs and glides. As well as all the advantages of an aerotow the motor glider student gets more of the flying by being able to practise his turns during the climbs. Moreover, the launch to 2,000 or 3,000 feet uses only a fraction of the fuel burned by a normal tow plane. Each flight on a motor glider releases another launch for a normal glider.

Learning to land is a near impossible problem when the students only get one glider flight per day, and even with a turn of three launches it is sometimes a problem. In a motor glider it is possible to make at least six landings per half-hour flight. Most of the motor gliders like the Falke are a little more difficult to land than a normal training glider because of the 'tail dragger' arrangement of the undercarriage which necessitates a fully held-off landing to avoid bouncing. The skills needed to hold off fully for a tail-down landing are definitely needed for the more advanced single-seater gliders which also have the 'tail dragger' arrangement. After the motor glider, the normal glider seems very easy to land.

Surprisingly, a few instructors still profess to doubt the value of this method of training. Few will dispute that it is easier to teach a student who has already done even a few hours of power flying. The motor glider student has the advantage of being able to learn to co-ordinate correctly with the stick and rudder. They can also learn the fundamentals of circuit planning and how to use the airbrakes. So, at worst, the student is getting some power experience in an aircraft which handles like a glider, glides like a glider and simulates one in most respects. There would certainly be no arguments if the trainer was a normal type of training glider fitted with a quiet engine for launching.

Other instructors fear that the student will rely on the engine to get them out of trouble. This could happen but is avoided by treating these aircraft as a glider once the engine has either been stopped altogether, or is throttled back and left idling at very low power.

It is an important principle that, when training, the engine is never used for convenience or to avoid difficult situations which a glider pilot would have had to deal with. For example there can be situations where, because of flying into strong sink, the glider must be turned in to land early, perhaps even cutting in ahead of another glider. If this situation arises on a flight in a motor glider, the engine must not be used. The engine should be stopped altogether for every flight at the later stages when the student is learning about planning and decision making.

It is indisputable that for advanced training, a motor glider is the only practical aircraft for teaching field selection and approaches without time-wasting retreives. It is also ideal for teaching map reading and even for advanced cross-country soaring.

Speed flying can be simulated by improving the glide performance with a small amount of power and using more power to artificially increase the rates of climb. In this way poor soaring conditions can be 'improved' and the more experienced pilots can be put under extra pressure so that their work-load is similar to racing on a good day.

Motor gliders are also excellent for practising final glides as this can be done on any day that the cloud base is high enough.

Problems with design

Of course our present motor gliders are not ideal for this work. They are not designed specifically for training and are compromises between having a passable glide performance and sufficient speed in level flight to satisfy the power pilot who wants to tour as well as soar.

In most of the present breed the rudder loads are far higher than on the majority of gliders, and since learning to use the rudder is one of the major problems for the student, this is not ideal. Fortunately this is not a difficult design problem. In some types the circling speeds are also unrealistically high and the larger radius of turn changes the conditions for the final turn and also for thermal soaring.

The other problem area is on the landing – not because of the diffi-culty in making good landings, although this may worry some of the less experienced instructors – but because the faster landing speeds caused by the higher wing loadings make it disastrous to make poor landings. Any bouncing on the relatively rough ground of most gliding sites is very likely to cause expensive damage. Everything is fine if the landings are good, but the higher speeds make the shocks of landings very much more severe than for a slower glider. It seems unlikely that the weight of these machines will be radically reduced. They either need a larger wing area or a higher lift aerofoil to reduce the touch-down speed and make them better for basic training.

Suggestions for improvement

One possibility would be to design a machine specifically for glider pilot training. The important features required are glider-like handling, that is high adverse yaw, light stick and rudder forces, glider-type airbrakes, a low stalling speed and the best rate of climb possible. The gliding performance is not so important because the glide can be 'improved' by leaving a small amount of power on during the descents. Above all, the aircraft must be rugged in order to reduce the risk of damage during bad landings. Since the gliding angle is not critical, this type of trainer would not be such a difficult design compromise as the present motor gliders.

With this type of aircraft the time spent climbing would be minimal and the task of teaching circuits and landings would be made quicker and easier. It would not be so economical for touring, but it might climb well enough to double as a tow plane.

Another practical alternative is the idea of attaching a 'power egg' to a standard two-seater glider. In this case the engine would not be retractable but could be removed altogether when not required. The drag caused by this kind of installation usually ruins the gliding performance but this can be overcome by leaving a little power during the glides. This has been tried several times and reports on an Australian Blanik two-seater fitted with an engine on a pylon above the wing showed it to have almost identical handling to the normal glider, making it perfect for training. It remains to be seen whether the noise level in the cockpits can be made low enough to be acceptable for normal instruction with this type of engine mounting.

Other problems with motor glider training

It is obvious that if the handling can be made similar to a normal glider, a motor glider must be superior for basic training where so much time can be spent on judgement training and on circuits and landings. However, motor glider training does have problems. For youth training schemes it has the disadvantage that, apart from the actual flying, there is very little for the student to do, unlike glider training where team-work and co-operation are essential and the majority of students are fully occupied.

In normal club use the motor glider may seem to encourage people to sit and wait for their turn to fly instead of helping with the other things which need doing at the glider launch point. A few people drop out when they move on to the gliders and find that they are expected to play their part with the ground handling and so on. Some would like to continue to fly motor gliders rather than move on to aerotowing or winch launching.

To be economical a motor glider needs to be fully utilised and this makes it unsuitable for a small club. It costs about twice as much as a normal glider to buy, making both the insurance and depreciation much more, and therefore it needs to be used a great deal to justify its expense.

The other major problem is that the instructors have to be of a high standard, both as pilots and instructors. A few seconds' inattention during a landing can result in expensive damage and the loss of the use of the aircraft during repairs is also costly.

When utilising the flying time efficiently the work-load of the instructor is far higher than on a glider or a normal powered aircraft. For example when teaching a group of five students on a week's course, I have frequently made seventy to eighty landings in a day. This kind of work-load is very tiring and is not every instructor's idea of how to spend a pleasant summer's afternoon. Compare this with the relaxed atmosphere at the glider launch point, making one or two launches per hour. However, the instructor certainly has his reward in seeing the rapid progress of the students on the motor glider.

Glider training may seem relatively inexpensive at a gliding club, but it is both expensive and time-consuming when it is done on a large scale. The motor glider can offer economic and efficient training on a large scale if that is required.

19 Parachuting

Expert parachutists tell us that safe parachuting is by no means difficult, but that to be sure of a safe landing you really need a short course of training together with a few practice jumps.

Assuming that you have neither the time nor the inclination to throw yourself out of a perfectly serviceable aeroplane just 'for the hell of it', it is worth thinking about how to increase your chances of being able to walk down to the local pub for a pint after landing instead of being carried off on a stretcher.

During the last war aircrews were given very little advice or training about parachuting, and about sixty per cent of all emergency drops resulted in some kind of injury, usually on the landing. There is no doubt that if you get out of the aircraft and pull the rip-cord you are almost certain to survive. But with just a little forethought and understanding the whole thing becomes far less dangerous.

Buying and looking after your parachute

First a few points about buying a parachute and looking after it. Perhaps the most important thing for gliding is to get one which is comfortable to wear in your particular cockpit. Make sure that when you are wearing it your straps do not press directly on the buckles of the parachute harness. Five hours of flying like that could be hell.

Modern glider packs are much thinner than the old ones but have the same sized canopies. Unless you are a very heavy person any normal chute will do. The more modern types can be steered but are not as manoeuvrable as the sport chutes.

The canopy will have the date of manufacturing stamped on it and most types have a life of eighteen to twenty years before they are scrapped. The value of the second-hand chute depends mainly on how old it is and so obviously you need to check this date. Perhaps the safest thing is to have it checked over and repacked by a qualified packer who will confirm the date and the general condition of the whole outfit.

Each parachute has a packing card to show when and by whom it has been packed. They should be repacked every three months. This involves 'pulling' the chute and hanging it up to dry out for several days before inspecting and repacking it. Parachutes should be kept in a proper bag in a dry place when not in use. Special care should be taken not to put it anywhere near direct heat or damp. If a chute gets wet do not dry it out on a hot radiator but get it repacked. A damp canopy will certainly delay the opening if not prevent it opening altogether. Keep parachutes away from oil and battery acid.

The daily inspection

1. Make sure the parachute is not overdue for repacking. (The packing card is usually kept in a little pocket under the backing pad and this will give the date it was last repacked.)
2. Inspect the harness for fraying and stains which might indicate contamination with oil or acid. Inspect the pack and make sure that no canopy or shroud lines are showing.
3. Make sure that the rip-cord handle and housing are secure and that the pins are fully home and are not bent. One pin is usually locked with thin red cotton to act as an indicator to show if the rip-cord handle has been partially pulled. The cotton should be intact.
4. Check each harness clip or the release box if one is fitted.

Carrying the parachute

How you carry a parachute is much more important than most pilots realise. Lift it and carry it as if it is a baby. Do not pick it up and carry it by the top harness straps. These are only stitched in place so that the stitching breaks as the parachute opens. A jerk can break the stitching, allowing shroud lines to appear. This will cause an uneven opening of the parachute or even a malfunction. Remember, unlike the sport parachutists you do not have a reserve chute.

Correct fitting

There are a number of slightly different types of parachute harness. Before tightening the straps get the pack as high as possible on your back. Do up the chest strap first. Adjusting and tightening the harness is important because if it is too loose you may do yourself an injury. Ideally the top buckles should be just at the top of your shoulder. You will be suspended by those straps if you use the chute. The other straps should be just tight enough to prevent you being able to stand upright. They will be much slacker once you are sitting down.

Emergency parachuting

Emergency parachuting can be divided into four stages: the decision to jump, the exit, the descent and the landing. It is interesting to note that the majority of fatalities occur during the exit (or lack of it) whereas almost all the injuries are the result of bad landings.

Deciding to jump

Unless you are a test pilot by far the most likely cause for baling out is having a collision. Collision is still the greatest single hazard in gliding. Obviously, if the glider goes completely out of control you should get out immediately. Remember that what may appear to be minor damage may result in a total structural failure by the time you are much lower down. If in doubt, get out!

Gliders are extremely strong and well built and it is very rare indeed for there to be a structural failure. At speeds below about 75 knots they are indestructable except in a tail slide. Experience has shown that even a disconnected aileron or an aileron control rod failure may leave the aircraft flyable if the rudder power is sufficient. Cases of the rudder hinges failing altogether have shown that, whereas in some cases the glider yaws and drops its nose violently, in others the glider has been flown down safely. Elevator damage or failure usually results in complete instability and is automatically a reason to jump. These types of problem are most likely to be the result of faulty rigging. Failing to connect up the controls correctly has been a persistent cause of accidents.

There have been cases when the pilot has stayed with the aircraft and flown it down only to lose control during the last few hundred feet. If you cannot see the damage or the glider is not fully controllable, get out.

No one should wear a parachute without understanding how to use it. If you are wearing parachutes in a two-seater you are responsible for briefing your student or passenger in what to do and how to do it.

The exit

You probably imagine that you would not have the nerve to bale out, but it has been shown that most people are quite up to it if the occasion arises.

First the cockpit canopy must be jettisoned. Operate the emergency release and the normal catch if necessary, and push the canopy up. Some canopies require pushing or kicking off as the air loads tend to keep them in place. The canopy should always go first because if you undo your straps you may be thrown against the canopy unable to release it. Make sure that you understand the jettison system of any glider that you fly and practise getting out of the cockpit quickly wearing your parachute.

It has been known for pilots to undo their parachute harness instead of their straps. So, look down, undo the straps and then get out as quickly as possible. You may be thrown out or alternatively be held in by the 'g' forces. It is advisable to try and leave on the inside of a spin. Pull yourself out and clear. Look for the rip-cord handle and pull it hard. If time allows, delay pulling the handle until you have had time to fall well clear of the aircraft. This part is a wonderful sensation! There is no feeling of falling and it is like lying on a feather bed. However, in free flight, unless you know enough to adopt a proper position, you may start to gyrate.

The necessary pull on the rip-cord handle is only an inch or so but it may take as much as 10–15kg (20–30lb). Usually it is far less than this. If necessary, use both hands and pull downwards and outwards away from you. Once pulled the handle comes free, there is a moment's delay and you will find yourself suspended by the parachute on your way down.

The descent

Look up and check that the parachute is fully developed and, if it is a club chute, check whether it has a red toggle on each of the 'risers' above your head. If so, you are lucky and have a steerable canopy. Pulling down on a toggle on one side will make the chute turn that way, so turn into wind to reduce the ground speed for the landing. As it is an emergency chute and not a free fall type the forward speed in no wind will only be a few miles an hour. Do not attempt to turn near the ground as you may oscillate and hit the ground with a sideways swipe.

With an ordinary non-steerable emergency chute, very little steering is possible. However, pulling down on the webs on one side will result in a slight change of direction. If the chute starts to swing badly milk the webs alternately to spill out some air.

The landing

It is often said that the shock of landing is like jumping off a ten foot wall. This is misleading. A more accurate description is that it is like jumping off a lorry moving at ten miles an hour. The real shock of the landing comes from the horizontal movement caused by the drift, and in most cases this is the cause of the injuries. The energy from the vertical and horizontal movement has got to be dissipated in a harmless manner as you fall over.

The first fundamental is to make sure that the feet and legs are held tightly together so that the initial shock is taken on the flat of both feet. The knees must be slightly bent and, as far as possible, relaxed rather than tensed ready for the shock. On no account should you attempt to land standing up. (That is only for sky-divers who have special chutes and lots of experience.) The hands should be above, holding the risers, and the elbows should be well tucked in.

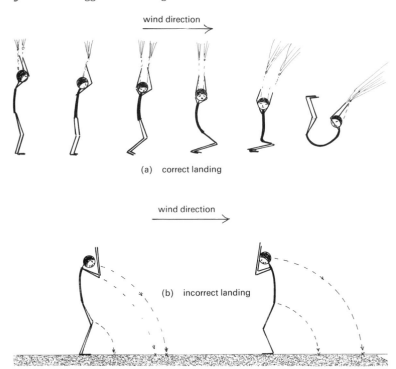

(a)   correct landing

(b)   incorrect landing

Parachute landings. (a)   Turn the lower body sideways if landing into or down wind. (b)   Landing forwards or backwards causes painful injuries.

The landing must never be made facing directly into or down wind. Imagine landing facing into wind drifting backwards. The landing shocks would be distributed on the feet, the bottom of the spine and then the head. (Ouch!) Landing drifting forwards, the shocks would be on the feet, the knees and then the face. These kinds of landings always hurt and often do permanent damage.

If it looks as though a forward or backward landing is going to occur, turn the lower part of the body sideways so that you land sideways with both feet together. With the knees slightly bent the shocks will then affect the feet, the side of the lower leg, the thigh and the back. This disippates the force without causing damage and is known in athletic circles as a shoulder roll. The beauty of this is that on impact all the force can be dispersed in a smooth, continuous movement along the least angular and therefore the least vulnerable parts of the body. This is well worth practising in the gym or on a bed. When you have got the idea you should be able to do it without hurting yourself on a normal carpet or on long grass. Make no mistake, practising these shoulder rolls could be very worth while if you do have to bale out.

After landing, the quickest way to deflate the canopy is to get up and run round it. This will make it topple and spill out the air. Alternatively, if you are being dragged along roll on to your stomach and pull in any shroud lines you can reach. Modern parachutes do not have any really quick way of releasing the harness so do not think you can do this to stop yourself being dragged along in a wind.

Unusual occurences

1. *Damage or faulty inflation of the canopy.* If the majority of the canopy appears to be all right, don't worry – you may only cause more trouble by messing about. If there is plenty of height, or if it is a serious looking defect, have one attempt at getting a full development by bringing the lift webs sharply together above your head.
2. *Landing in trees.* This is not so dangerous as it sounds. The recommended practice is now to keep the legs tightly together ready for a possible normal landing in case you fall between or right through the trees, and to cover your face with your arms. Wait for help – it would be a pity to break your neck after getting out safely. It is useful to know that each of the thin nylon shroud lines has a strength of over 200kg (450lb) and so is ample to take your weight.
3. *Landing in water.* Do not attempt to undo the harness until you are down. Remember, the water may be shallow in which case a normal feet together, knees bent landing is vital. Try to get the harness off quickly as you may be dragged along in a wind. Do not panic if you are under the canopy; it is porous and will let the air through for breathing.
4. *Jumping out in cloud.* Big clouds can have very strong updrafts and it is possible to have a long flight on a parachute if it opens in good lift. It would be nice to be able to advise making a delayed drop, but I am doubtful that this is practical on a first jump. The best advice is to avoid big clouds unless you are really competent at cloud flying. A modern glider out of control in cloud is almost certain to get to very high speeds, and if it flutters you will need your chute.

How low is it safe to jump?

This decision must depend a great deal on just how dangerous it would be to stay with the glider. The time taken for the parachute to open depends on your speed at the time of pulling the rip-cord. At low speeds the opening is slower and therefore takes up more height. During the war there were a number of cases of aircrews falling out of aircraft without parachutes and landing in snow or on slopes. There was even a case where a German airman fell into the mud in the Bristol Channel with very minor injuries! You probably have a good chance of surviving if you are out by 500 feet when you pull that rip-cord.

Will it ever happen to you?

On average there is one bale out from a glider every two years in the United Kingdom, and most are due to collisions and/or keeping an inadequate look-out. The moral is clear.

The odds are greatly against needing your chute, but it is better to be safe than sorry.

Saving your glider or your skin

Supposing you found yourself flying a badly damaged glider and were apparently just able to keep control. Would you try to get it down or bale out?

When faced with such a decision, make sure you do not waste valuable seconds making up your mind. Seconds like these might cost you your life, so it's well worth while spending a few minutes considering things beforehand.

Obviously, if the glider is uncontrollable the sooner you leave it the better. But what if you think that perhaps you could get the glider down?

Uppermost in my thoughts when my time came was the story of the Prefect pilot who, after a collision in cloud, kept control all the way down to the last few hundred feet, only to spin in and be seriously hurt. Nobody will thank you for staying with the glider if it is reduced to scrap by the landing. Therefore, if there is any doubt about keeping control a decision must be made while there is still enough height to jump safely.

It is embarrassing to have to ask your student to jump – but how would you feel if you were flying with an inexperienced passenger? It would be still more embarrassing if you happened to be using your parachute as a cushion and had not yet done up the harness, or if you had not explained to your passenger how to use the parachute.

A narrow escape

The incident in which I was involved happend when I was flying with a student in a Bocian high-performance two-seater. We had gone into a shallow dive, recovering from a rather sloppy chandelle, when there was a roar as the rear canopy slid back, followed by a loud bang as it hit the tail plane. Looking back, I could see that most of the tail plane on one side was missing, leaving only the rear spar and elevator.

We were flying at about 1,700 feet at a steady speed of around 50–55 knots and heading towards the airfield. The elevator control seemed to be jammed solid but the ailerons were normal. The airbrake caused no change of trim, and the glider seemed to be stable.

I had all the arguments worked out, and it did not take long to make the decision. 'No elevator control means no levelling out for the landing and therefore a fair risk of broken ankles in the front cockpit. If during any turn the nose drops the glider may continue to dive, and this may happen when it is too late to jump. This is an unacceptable risk, so we must jump for it.'

By this time we were almost directly over the airfield and the centre of attention. I doubt whether any of the people on the ground had ever before heard a pilot give the order to get out or seen such an escape so clearly.

The front canopy was jettisoned and, held by its retaining cable, struck me hard on the head before embedding itself in the starboard wing root. By this time I was anxious about our height, so I unstrapped and leaned forward to read the altimeter and also to make sure that my student had found his rip-cord handle. (We have at least two different types of harness with the rip-cord handles in different places, and I was worried he might not find it.) At 1,200 feet my student left without further ado.

This caused an astounding change of trim. The glider reared up steeply and I got out hurriedly. I immediately found myself sprawled on the port wing and held there by the glider rolling rapidly to the right. I had just decided to make an effort to push myself off when the rolling stopped and I found myself falling away freely, watching the Bocian which had settled down into a gentle inverted turn.

I pulled the rip-cord and, slightly to my surprise at the time, found myself parachuting down with my student a few hundred feet above me and the Bocian still inverted but far enough away to forget it. Looking down, I found myself drifting slightly towards the woods, but there was no time to experiment or even to look up and see where the shroud lines were. I was rather relieved to realise that I would land in the trees, and I lifted my knees up and covered my head for the landing.

There I was, fifteen feet up and hardly scratched. I shouted to my student to stay where he was and not on any account to release his harness, believing that he must be in the trees nearby. However, he was safely down on solid ground.

The most frightening part was getting down from the tree. This was accomplished with the help of our winch driver and the club members.

Summary of lessons learned

1. It happened to me and it could happen to you.
2. Think about the circumstances in which you might have to jump, and have your actions planned out beforehand. If you do not decide quickly you may waste valuable time and reduce your chances of survival.
3. Don't carry a parachute; *wear* it, and make sure you and your passenger know how to use it.
4. Practise getting out of your glider quickly with your parachute on.

Most fatalities occur because of failing to get out in time.

5.   Remember, release the canopy first, then the straps and then get out.

6.   Be prepared for the glider pitching violently nose-up as you or your passenger leave.

7.   Try to delay pulling for a few seconds to get well clear of the glider or the pieces of it that remain. Pilots have been pursued by pieces of the glider while parachuting down. If possible, get well clear before pulling the rip-cord, but do not delay too long. (A simple sum showed that another five seconds' delay and this book would never have been written!)

8.   Check the canopy and look to see if steering toggles are fitted. If they are, steer round into wind to avoid the drift.

9.   Prepare for the landing. Grasp the lift webs, tuck your elbows in, keep your knees bent and knees and feet tightly together.

10.   Trees are usually very safe landing places – but wait for help.

11.   Turn the lower parts of your body to allow a sideways landing. Do not land facing directly into or down wind.

12.   Try to make a shoulder roll on touch-down.

13.   Run round the chute or pull on any shroud lines to deflate the canopy.

Remember, the parachute is your friend if you treat it well. If you do not, a cushion is just as much use and much more comfortable! Once the decision to jump has been made, I assure you that parachuting is a very pleasant experience.

Appendix A
Conversion tables

Metres		Feet	Kilo-metres		Miles	Kilo-grammes		Pounds
0.305	1	3.281	1.609	1	0.621	0.454	1	2.205
0.610	2	6.562	3.219	2	1.243	0.907	2	4.409
0.914	3	9.843	4.828	3	1.864	1.361	3	6.614
1.219	4	13.123	6.438	4	2.485	1.814	4	8.818
1.524	5	16.404	8.047	5	3.107	2.268	5	11.023
1.829	6	19.685	9.656	6	3.728	2.722	6	13.228
2.134	7	22.966	11.265	7	4.350	3.175	7	15.432
2.438	8	26.247	12.875	8	4.971	3.629	8	17.687
2.743	9	29.528	14.848	9	5.592	4.082	9	19.842
3.048	10	32.808	16.093	10	6.214	4.536	10	22.046
6.906	20	65.617	32.187	20	12.427	9.072	20	44.092
7.620	25	82.021	40.234	25	15.534	11.340	25	55.116
15.240	50	164.042	80.467	50	31.069	22.680	50	110.231
30.480	100	328.084	160.924	100	62.137	45.359	100	220.462

SPEED CONVERSION SCALE

KNOTS	MPH	KM/H	FT/SEC
10	10	10	10
20	20	20	20
30	30	30	30
40	40	40	40
50	50	50	50
60	60	60	60
70	70	70	70
80	80	80	80
90	90	90	90
100	100	100	100
110	110	110	110
120	120	120	120
130	130	130	130
140	140	140	140
150	150	150	150
	160	160	160
	170	170	170
		180	180
		190	190
		200	200
		210	210
		220	220
		230	230
		240	240
		250	250
		260	
		270	

RATE OF CLIMB CONVERSION SCALE

KNOTS	METRES PER SEC	FT/MIN	FT/SEC	KM/H	MPH
1	1	100	1–10	1–10	1–22
2	2	200			
3	3	300			
4	4	400			
5	5	500			
6	6	600			
7	7	700			
8	8	800			
9	9	900			
10	10	1000			
11		1100			
12		1200			
13		1300			
14		1400			
15		1500			
16		1600			
17		1700			
18		1800			
19		1900			
		2000	33	36	

CONVERSION FACTORS

	To convert	into	Multiply by
Distances			
	Metres	Feet	3.281
	Feet	Metres	0.3048
	Centimetres	Inches	0.394
	Inches	Centimetres	2.540
	Kilometres	Miles	0.6214
	Miles	Kilometres	1.609
	Kilometres	Nautical Miles	0.5396
	Nautical Miles	Kilometres	1.853
	Miles	Nautical Miles	0.869
	Nautical Miles	Miles	1.151
Speeds			
	Kilometres per hour	Miles per hour	0.6214
	Miles per hour	Kilometres per hour	1.609
	Km/h	Knots	0.5396
	Knots	Km/h	1.853
	Metres per second	Feet per second	3.281
	Feet per second	Metres per second	0.3048
	M.p.h.	Knots	0.869
	Knots	M.p.h.	1.151
	Feet per minute	Metres per second	.00508
	Metres per second	Feet per minute	196.85
	Knots	Metres per second	0.515
	Metres per second	Knots	1.944
Areas			
	Square metres	Square feet	10.764
	Square feet	Square metres	0.093
	Square centimetres	Square inches	0.155
	Square inches	Square centimetres	6.451
Weights			
	Kilogrammes	Pounds	2.205
	Pounds	Kilogrammes	0.454
Wing loadings and tyre pressures			
	Kg per square metre	Lb per square foot	0.205
	Lb per square foot	Kg per square metre	4.882
	Lb per square inch	Kg per square centimetre	0.07
	Kg per square centimetre	Lb per square inch	14.3

Weight of Water

1 Imperial gallon = 4.546 litres	= 1.2 US gallons,	weighs 10 lb
1 litre = 0.22 Imperial gallons	= 0.264 US gallons,	weighs 2.2 lb
1 US gallon = 3.8 litres	= 0.83 Imperial gallons,	weighs 8.3 lb

Useful addresses

BGA (British Gliding Association)
Kimberley House, Vaughan Way, Leicester LE1 4SG. Tel: (0533) 531051.

SSA (Soaring Society of America)
PO Box E, Hobbs, New Mexico 88241. Tel: (505) 392–1177.

GFA (Gliding Federation of Australia)
GFA Secretariat, 130 Wirraway Road, Essendon Airport 3041 (Melbourne), Australia. Tel: (03) 379 7411 or 4629.

New Zealand Gliding Association
KIWI Private Bag, Taurange, New Zealand.

Index